Impoverished
STATE OF MIND
Thinking Outside da Block

Impoverished
STATE OF MIND
Thinking Outside da Block

TORRI STUCKEY

COVER THREE PUBLISHING

OAK FOREST, IL

Impoverished State of Mind: Thinking Outside da Block

Published by Cover Three Publishing
P.O. Box 947, Oak Forest, IL 60452-0947
www.cover3publishing.com

ISBN: 978-0-615-65959-6 (pbk.)

Printed in the United States of America
2012—First Edition

The names of some individuals in this book have been changed in order to protect their privacy.

Edited by Dave Krump
Interior design by Matt Duckett
Indexed by Laura Shelley

Please send all feedback to:
isom@cover3publishing.com

To all my young people in the hood (from Mudville to Marcy), I know when you look outside life can seem uninspiring, but keep the faith; I'm living proof that dreams do come true.

To the two men that inspired me in life and in death...

My man, O (Otis), you sparked the flame. I'm doing my best to carry the torch.

My hero, Rocky, the strength you showed daily will last me an eternity.

Rest in peace

CONTENTS

"Real Talk"

As a youngin' I never read books, so I applaud your effort. You've managed to successfully open this book, so the hardest part is already over…at least for you. On the other hand, I have the extremely difficult task of keeping your attention and convincing you that this book is more important than some of the other activities that occupy your time—listening to music, watching TV, or engaging in social media. I will do my best, but it will require a mutual effort on your part.

There will be some topics that are more appealing than others, but I challenge you to stay the course. This book is not a page longer than it has to be. I kept it as short as humanly possible without sacrificing the message. Every page of every chapter plays a vital role and has a unique purpose. It's like piecing together a puzzle; you can jump around to different sections and get a partial view of the image, but to see the full picture you must put all the pieces together.

Depending on your age, some of the topics may seem a little advanced. You might say to yourself, "I'm still young. Why do I need to worry about all this right now?" If you go outside and look around, the answer surrounds you. If your ultimate goal is to rise above poverty, you will need to be forward thinking. This book is meant to stimulate your mind and start your progress out of poverty.

Before you begin this journey, I want you to stop and ask yourself, "Why am I reading this book?" Some of you were probably given this book by a teacher, family member, friend or social worker. Others found the title or book cover interesting enough to open and begin reading. No matter how you arrived at this point, you need to make a decision—right now—whether to stay or go. If you choose to stay, you will not regret it. By the time you finish this book, you will have a new outlook on life.

You will learn new truths about yourself. In some instances, you will have to re-educate yourself about false beliefs of the past—things you were taught in the hood that are inconsistent with the beliefs of the rest of the world.

What you are exposed to growing up in the hood is not "real life," it's "hood life." The kind of lives people live in the absence of money, education and other bare necessities. Most people living in this country do not live this deprived way of life. The United States is one of the richest countries in the world. People who live in poverty are the minority, not the majority.

Growing up in the hood, you live sheltered from the outside world. We usually reserve the term "sheltered" for rich kids who live in mansions with a butler and a maid. In reality, poor kids are also sheltered. The difference is that rich kids are sheltered from harm and exposed to fine arts like ballet, tap, theater and piano lessons; while poor kids are sheltered from good and introduced to drugs, gangs, guns and prostitution by the time they reach puberty. At the same age you witnessed your first drive-by, the children of wealthy Americans performed Beethoven's 5th Symphony for a room filled with camcorders.

The problem with growing up in an impoverished environment is that you think that because you've witnessed a few drive-bys—maybe sold a few drugs—you've seen it all and been through it all. You wrote the book on life. You have the world all figured out. You understand exactly the way the game works. Somehow your past hardship attempts to legitimize you as an expert on life. As a result, you assume you know more about life than everyone else—Lord knows I did. In reality, you know little about the world as a whole. Our only knowledge of it is the distorted view that is revealed to us during our coming-of-age in the hood.

Back in 1994, Chicago made national headlines when eleven-year-old Robert "Yummy" Sandifer was murdered. The murder of Yummy gained attention from the local news, but what captured a national audience was the lifestyle this young boy led up to his death. While he was a victim of murder, he was far from innocent. At the tender age of eleven he had already committed 23 felonies and 5 misdemeanors. Young Yummy was involved in gang and drug activity, and associated with two shootings—one resulting in the death of Shavon Dean, a 14 year old girl.

It is suspected that Yummy was killed by his own gang members. As the investigation surrounding the murder of Shavon Dean intensified, Yummy became a liability. Fellow gang members feared that if caught Yummy might implicate them to the police. Weeks after the shooting, Yummy was found dead in a muddy pool of blood near a viaduct, two gunshot wounds in the back of his head—execution style. He was only a young boy, but at eleven years of age he had already succumbed to the allure of the streets.

Even though you're young, most of you have started paving your life's path. Living in the hood, you've already picked up some bad habits—ones that if left undetected could steer you in the wrong direction. Your destination may be unclear, but every decision you make is indeed shaping your path.

Some of you have dropped out of high school and started selling drugs. It's highly likely that you will eventually spend years in prison. Maybe you consider yourself a player, dating multiple girls, and are well on your way to having six kids by five different women. Some of you flirtatious young ladies will unfortunately be on the other end of the equation—six kids by five different men. And so the cycle of poverty continues...

The same issues—drugs, gangs, lack of education, teenage pregnancy—have been plaguing impoverished black communities for decades. These problems are not new and you're not the first person that has had to face them. I was approached almost daily by crack addicts looking for drugs. Every day I had to choose between staying broke and doing what was right, or sacrifice my morals for a pair of new sneakers and some petty cash.

From one decade to the next, the situation might change, but the root issue itself will remain the same. Instead of the dope boys slangin' crack, they might start pushing Ecstasy. Instead of being robbed for your Jordans, you might get stuck-up for your Lebrons. As medical science evolves, you might go from having multiple abortions to taking several morning-after pills. The form of the issues might change, but the core issues have and will remain the same.

If the issues are the same and they have been outlined repeatedly, "Why is poverty still such a major problem in the black community?" It's either because people refuse to listen, or they don't fully understand. That said, my goal is not to convince those determined to live the street life to change their ways. It's to provide those who want to succeed in life with knowledge and understanding that will help them along the way.

Growing up my grandmother would say to me, "Boy, you don't believe fat meat greasy." As a child, I had no clue what she meant. It took me years to figure out that not believing fat meat is greasy meant that I had to learn things the hard way. I often challenged my grandmother's views. She attempted to pass on her words of wisdom and guidance, but I wanted to do things my way. As a result, I learned many tough lessons in ways that hurt. Sometimes we have to face some pain before we will face reality. If you find yourself unwilling to entertain an alternative thought process, tuck this book away and revisit it in a year. The harsh realities in this book will not change, but hopefully over the next twelve months, you will experience some challenges in life that will open your mind and allow you to better receive the message.

In the context of poverty, it has been said time and time again that "education is the key to success," yet impoverished minorities continue to drop out of high school at a staggering rate. This indicates to me that I am not alone—as there are many other people who also "don't believe fat meat greasy." That thought process has to change.

One common theme you will recognize throughout this book is

"change." Change in your attitude. Change in your thought process. Change in your approach to life. No one gets to choose the family situation or environment they are born into, but you can choose how you respond to your circumstances. If you were born into poverty, ultimately it is your choice whether or not you stay impoverished.

There are a thousand reasons why you could remain in poverty, but you have to find one reason why you shouldn't. Poverty can be defeated. In order to do so, you have let go of all the mistakes and disappointments of the past. You must keep your focus forward and make every effort to move towards the future. Most importantly, all the self-handicapping and self-pity has to end—right now! The time is over for feeling sorry for yourself and playing the role of victim.

If you were born into poverty…I'm sorry. If you live in poverty… I'm sorry. If you live in a single-parent home…I'm sorry. If you live in the projects…I'm sorry. If you live in a trailer park…I'm sorry. If you are homeless…I'm sorry. If you sleep on roof tops…I'm sorry. If you live with roaches and rats…I'm sorry. If you're a ward of the state…I'm sorry. If you've been physically abused…I'm sorry. If you've been sexually abused…I'm sorry. If you've been verbally abused…I'm sorry. If your mother neglects you…I'm sorry. If your father disowns you…I'm sorry. If you're without food…I'm sorry. If you're without clothes… I'm sorry. If you're struggling to make ends meet…I'm sorry. If your family is on welfare…I'm sorry. If your parents are drug addicts…I'm sorry. If your parents are alcoholics…I'm sorry. If you don't know your father…I'm sorry. If your father is in prison…I'm sorry. If your sister overdosed on drugs…I'm sorry. If your brother was killed by gang violence…I'm sorry. If you're a teenage mother…I'm sorry. If you're a teenage father…I'm sorry. If you dropped out of high school…I'm sorry. If you can't find a job…I'm sorry. If you can't afford college… I'm sorry. If you're selling drugs "just to survive"…I'm sorry. If you've been shot multiple times…I'm sorry. If you have a record…I'm sorry. If you've been incarcerated…I'm sorry. If the public school system failed you…I'm sorry. If the white man has oppressed you…I'm sorry.

If you etcetera, etcetera, etcetera...I AM SORRY!

That will be the last time you hear me express sympathy for anyone's situation. Now that we got that out of the way, we can begin this journey of EMPOWERMENT!

1

I.S.O.M.

Impoverished State of Mind: a mindset developed by a false sense of blackness that associates being poor (and all that it entails) with being African American (2): the psychological condition caused by the real or perceived absence of necessary means or essentials (3): a mindset developed from living in poverty and being exposed to deviant behavior

You were a kid once—innocent, naïve and trusting of everyone. A time when you would leap off of furniture into your father's arms, trusting he would catch you and not let you fall. As a kid you would hold your mother's hand as you crossed the street, trusting that she would guide you and keep you away from harm. This trust enabled you to live free, without a care in the world, but the streets robbed us of this innocence. The sights and sounds of our favorite cartoons were replaced by terribly negative images.

What is merely a reflection of poverty has become your perception of reality—or life as you know it. This misperception has shaped your way of thinking and altered your approach to life. It causes you to assume false limitations—which result in underachievement—and forces others to risk their lives selling drugs out of hopelessness and desperation. It is the reason so many young people leave this earth well before their time. This is the definition and result of an *Impoverished State of Mind*.

If you're anything like me, your first question is, "Who are you?" and "What gives you the audacity to write a book about poverty?" I was born in poverty and lived in poverty for more than eighteen years of my life. As a result, I suffered from an impoverished state of mind. But at thirty years of age, I can humbly and graciously say that I no longer live in poverty and I've conquered my impoverished state of mind. I have a degree from Northwestern University. I run my own small publishing company and I enjoy every moment of it. I say this not to impress you, but to impress upon you that I have been where you are. And I've made it to where you're hopefully trying to go—a place of happiness and prosperity. The road I traveled to reach this point was rough. There were some dead ends and wrong turns. However, it's a road I believe most can appreciate and more importantly learn from.

I chose to write this book now because I've reached a stage in my life where I feel I have a voice that people will listen to. Not because of where I am, but because of what I have overcome. It was also important to me to write this book while I'm not too far removed from poverty—both physically and financially. The memories are still very vivid in my mind. I can remember what I felt as a teenager, wondering how I would make it out, or if I would make it out.

I had many people guide me along the way and provide a positive influence in my life. My goal is to provide similar support and direction to young men and women who are currently battling with the stresses of life in the hood.

When you live in poverty, you are taught to believe life is one way and one way only. You never challenge that belief system because those you interact with have a similar viewpoint. It's not until you gain exposure to the outside world (i.e., the world beyond the hood) and start to see another side of life that you begin to question your thoughts.

Very few individuals have the opportunity to live in one of the poorest communities in their state and attend one of the most prestigious universities in the nation. I was blessed with that opportunity. Through that experience I discovered there were some beliefs I had developed as a child that were fundamentally wrong. These same beliefs were the foundation on which I shaped my perspective. As my outlook started to change it made me wonder, "What else have I been wrong about?" So I began digging. The hole grew deeper and wider. Through a sincere and objective analysis of myself, I began to realize the magnitude of ignorance and backwards thinking that existed within me and subsequently throughout impoverished communities. Due to the lack of education and limited exposure to the outside world, these false beliefs are passed down through generations until somehow the cycle is broken.

Sometimes the cycle is broken when a family member graduates from college. Not only due to the positive financial impact that having a bachelor's degree provides, attending college also removes you from the hood environment and places you in an atmosphere that encourages you to seek knowledge. College exposes you to new cultures and new ideas that develop a new ideology. But like everything else new thoughts are a choice. Some who graduate from college maintain an impoverished mentality. They were exposed to a different way of thinking, but resisted the change. Or they remained in their comfort zone and failed to take advantage of the diversity that college life has to offer.

I was the first person in my immediate family to graduate from college. When I came back home, I was a different person. Misconceptions I overlooked in the past stuck out like a sore thumb. For example, the concept of "talkin' white." Growing up in the hood, I can remember hearing black people referring to other blacks, those who spoke proper English and enunciated their words, as "talkin' white." As a result, I would refer to them the same. When I got to college, every black person around me talked white. It was like I had moved to another country and no one there spoke my language. I remember one of my white teammates would often say to me, "T-Stuck you talk funny" I would laugh and reply, "So do you."

This issue of "talkin' white" is not racial—as the phrase suggests—it's a socioeconomic issue. Blacks who live in poverty are typically uneducated. This results in the use of broken English. Living in the hood, I only interacted with blacks from the lower-class. However all black people are not from the hood. There are plenty affluent black people who are educated and use proper English. Thus, characteristics of the hood—urban slang, broken English, vulgar language—do not embody all black people. There is a fundamental difference between being black and being poor. But it is extremely hard to differentiate the two because they've been synonymous with one another for so many years.

In college, the distinction between race and social class became starkly apparent, as I was one of the few students (black or white) from the lower-class. Hearing well-spoken black students triggered a negative response in my mind. I perceived it as an exaggerated attempt to act white. This made me fight even harder to preserve my strong sense of blackness—or what I perceived as blackness—so I sagged my pants a lil' harder, tipped my fitted cap a lil' lower and kept on moving.

My plan was to get my education, play football and keep to myself. The only problem with that plan is that I wasn't a Monk. At some point I would have to at least interact with the black girls on campus. When I did, it wasn't long before I realized that these black people were not "talkin' white." They were educated. And it was my own ignorance that caused me to believe in this "talkin' white" nonsense for so long.

There were many other views I had to re-educate myself about— beliefs I used to live by without ever questioning the truth of them (blackness, interracial dating, music, etc). This "re-education" had little to do with school, or my major for that matter. I used college as a lens to look out into the world that had been hidden from me for so many years.

Northwestern provided a great platform, as there were students on campus from thirty-three different countries. I majored in Communications, but all I ever studied was people (I probably should have been a Sociology major). I had the pleasure of sharing dorm rooms with students from all walks of life. My first roommate was a second generation Nigerian from an upper middle-class city in Ohio. My second roommate was a second generation Japanese from Iowa with dual citizenship and my last roommate was a Canadian from the province of Quebec with Caribbean heritage.

One aspect of college that is extremely different from high school is that when school is adjourned, you don't jump on a bus or in a car and go home. You are there 24/7. I would argue that the majority of the learning experience occurs after class is over. I can remember many nights, sitting around with my roommates discussing our backgrounds and sharing stories about our youth. We all had unique experiences—which gave each of us different perspectives on life. It was enlightening to listen to all the different outlooks on the world. I learned a great deal from those conversations. They taught me to stop believing the world was flat—so to speak.

I started to scrutinize my beliefs. If there was no real justification behind one of my beliefs, I stopped subscribing to it. It was alarming to witness the amount of thoughts that were altered; so many of my core beliefs changed that it shook my foundation. This was a time of great insecurity—as I attempted to uncover my true self. Once I made it through the process, I vowed never to take my beliefs for granted again.

Each day I strive to gain a deeper understanding of myself and of the world. In order to be myself, I must first understand who I am. People do not exist in a vacuum. No one believes something "just because." You believe something because you learned it as an adolescent or as a child from a parent, teacher or some other outside influence.

Instead of being from the hood, imagine your ascribed status placed you in warfare—much like the child soldiers in Africa—where from the point in which you were able to stand, someone handed you a semi-automatic weapon and told you to fight. How much would your behavior patterns change?

As the dynamics surrounding a person change, so do the thought patterns. When submerged into a society of "survival of the fittest," no matter how reluctant you are you will learn to survive by any means necessary!

It is not in a child's nature to want to kill another human being, but warlords brainwash children to believe violence is the way of the world. Similar to the dope boys in the hood who have been conditioned to believe that selling drugs is a healthy alternative to school or working a legal job, the young in other nations have been corrupted by fools with deadly agendas.

We are all products of our environment. That is a fact, but there are certain characteristics of a person that are innate. For instance, if from birth a child was raised by wolves, the child would act like a wolf. All the cultural elements of wolves would be reflected through the child's behavioral patterns. By the same token, if the same child was raised by pigs instead, the child's behavior would reflect the pigs' way of life. These are all learned behaviors that can fluctuate from culture to culture. The characteristics of the child that remain consistent, whether being raised by pigs or wolves, are the true essence of the child and are independent of all environmental influences. That's why you can have two brothers raised in the same housing projects, by the same single mother, and one become a doctor and the other a street pharmacist.

This book will challenge you to separate the product (you) from the environment and take a deeper look into the characteristics of your individual identity. Who am I really? Why do I think the way that I think? Why do I dress the way that I dress? Why do I talk the way that I talk? Why do I desire the materials (shoes, clothes, jewelry, tattoos) that I desire?

Even though we are products of our environment, we are all unique. Our minds process and interpret images differently. What some may find appealing, others will find grotesque. While some of you will be addicted to street life, others will find it unsatisfying and set out on a quest for a more fulfilling life. Those of you thirsting for more out of life, I will do my best to assist you on your journey.

In order to do so you have to be willing to challenge the status-quo. You must abandon what you have accepted as truth and seek truth for yourself. Don't believe something just because I say so, or society says so, see for yourself. Develop your own opinion.

This book will force you to think outside da block. When I say, "outside da block," I mean there is a world that exists outside the streets of the hood, and to succeed in that world, you will have to expand your thoughts beyond the knowledge and understanding you gained growing up in the hood—or form a new ideology altogether. It may even require you to denounce your parents' thoughts and beliefs and create your own. The truth is if your mother or father grew up in poverty and have had limited exposure to the outside world, no matter their age, chances are they still have an impoverished state of mind— to some degree.

As a result, parents can unintentionally be their child's worst enemy. As a child, we take on our parents' personae. Their beliefs become our beliefs until we reach an age of understanding and can develop our own. Even then, we are still a reflection of our parents and the way we were raised. If you were raised in a household where your parents were outwardly racist, you probably have similar beliefs—or did at some point.

There are certain characteristics and fundamental beliefs associated with living in poverty. If you grew up in a household where your parents displayed an impoverished state of mind, you likely embraced the same beliefs. Concepts like thriftiness or saying, "I can't afford it." When in reality, if you budgeted correctly, you possibly could afford "it." Rather than say, "I can't afford it" I'd prefer you simply say, "I choose not to spend my money on it." This is a more empowering statement. It puts you in control of the situation—rather than be governed by your finances. Some might argue, "same difference," but this approach will help train your mind to reject this impoverished way of thinking.

I give you permission to challenge some of the lessons your parents taught you. Take nothing for granted. Scrutinize everything. Question your parents' theories and principles. It might be met with resistance at first, but as long as you remain respectful any responsible parent will comply. Probing questions are an essential part of your maturation process. They are necessary for you to transition to the next stage in your life. Thus, parents should embrace these questions wholeheartedly.

Along with their misguided beliefs, some of your parents are setting bad examples. If you were never shown the correct way, how do you know if your parent is setting a good example or not? The answer to that question remains unclear, but there are some obvious signs that would suggest that your parent is setting bad examples. For instance, if your father is still gang related, or if you're often left home alone because your mother is out partying with her girlfriends.

If your parents are still living in the hood, it is not by accident. It's because they either enjoy living impoverished, or when the opportunity to escape presented itself they failed to seize the moment. For most, I believe it was the latter.

There was a crucial turning point in your parents' lives when they made the decision to rise above poverty, or live in it for the foreseeable future. It more than likely happened during their high school years. Your father made the decision to drop out of school, or he began selling drugs. Your mother became pregnant, or she decided to work rather than go to college. This decision forever changed their lives and yours for years to come.

At the time, your parents were young and did not understand the consequences of their actions. You see them now, as they have grown older—possibly grayer—through the eyes of a child. But please understand that they looked quite similar to you when they made their decision to stay in poverty—same youthful smile, same attitude.

The decisions your parents made are their decisions. You do not have to follow in their footsteps, but if you're not careful that is exactly what you will do. If you don't believe me, just look around you at all the generations of families still living in poverty—from grandmother to granddaughter. It's because too many children take on the impoverished (hood) mentality of their parents instead of creating their own identity. You had no hand in the choices they made. In fact, you were probably not even born yet. Your slate is clean, but there comes a time in every child's life, during the transition from adolescence to young adult, where you have to take ownership over your future and decide whether or not you are going to remain in poverty. At this point in life, no matter how negligent your parents were, or how ill-equipped you feel, your success or failure will fall squarely on your shoulders. If you do not succeed please don't blame your parents...blame yourself!

I learned at a very early age not to focus on the circumstances beyond my control. I cannot change your family situation or the environment you were born into—neither can you. All we can do is pick up our swords and battle. The odds are stacked against you. The environment that you live in is not conducive to positive growth. But with a lot of effort and a little bit of guidance, you can and will lift yourself out of poverty.

My goal is not to turn you bitter towards your parents. Poverty is a vicious cycle that repeats itself generation after generation. Your mother likely followed in your grandmother's footsteps. Your grandmother likely followed in your great grandmother's footsteps and so forth... Prior to the 1950s, the majority of African Americans lived in poverty. To add insult to injury, all but a tiny handful of blacks were effectively excluded from occupations with sufficient income to enable them to rise above poverty.

Truthfully, this problem was set in motion hundreds of years ago when the first slave ships crossed the Atlantic. The impoverished mentality is a complex residual effect caused by hundreds of years of oppression and racial discrimination that African Americans have had to overcome.

African Americans are a very resilient race of people. We can learn to adapt to any environment or situation we are faced with—no matter how difficult. When slaves were given the leftover scraps from hogs, they took what was supposed to be scrap food, gave it a little love, and turned it into a main course—hence the creation of soul food (neck bones, pig feet, chitterlings, etc.).

It is believed that Penguins derived from a species of birds that could fly. Due to their aquatic environment, Penguins had to adapt in order to survive. Over time their wings transformed into flippers. This evolution gave Penguins the ability to swim fast after prey, but rendered their wings (flippers) useless for flight.

What if I told you we, as African Americans, derived from a lineage of people that could fly (well mentally anyway)? What if I said the minds of our ancestors once soared high above Mount Kilimanjaro? But their minds were snatched out of the sky, bodies bound with shackles and enslaved—mentally and physically—for over 350 years. Over time we lost our ability to fly. We evolved—to no fault of our own—into a race of inferior, uneducated and impoverished people, merely striving to make it through the day.

We used to refer to it as a slave mentality. With more than a hundred and fifty years separating slavery from present day, there are few blacks who can truly identify with that past. But many African Americans can identify with being poor—a byproduct of slavery. That's why the mentality has transformed from a slave mentality to an impoverished state of mind. Today young impoverished African Americans identify more with the hood than the struggle. But the projects are not our birthplace. We have a rich history of growth and progress that stretches beyond the borders of America into the epicenter of the African Diaspora. This unparalleled history has led us to where we are today.

We have come a long way from slavery and the disparities of our past. This is a new day in America. The civil liberties our grandparents and great grandparents struggled to attain their entire lives, we inherited as a birth right. As a result, we don't have to live impoverished with established limitations. We can choose to take advantage of these privileges and change our fate.

We live in a democracy, meaning with the right opportunity, even the poorest man can turn his rags into riches. We see this often with lottery winners, but there are hundreds of other examples of ordinary people who were given an opportunity and became successful architects, engineers, physicians, attorneys, principals, and politicians.

Most notably, this country elected its first African American president, Barack Obama. I was hopeful this would happen during my lifetime, but I thought I would be well into my fifties before it occurred. Giving an African American the opportunity to be the Commander-in-Chief of the United States of America is proof of the strides we (Americans) have made as a society.

The one thing that stands out in my mind from Barack Obama's entire presidential campaign is his victory speech. It was a celebratory speech, but it was also a reality check.

"We have come so far. We have seen so much. But there's so much more to do." Obama said.

He could have been referring to the current economic crisis or the war in Iraq. As an African American, I interpreted it also as a message to the black community—especially since he made several references to the Civil Rights Movement.

There is tremendous responsibility and expectation that comes along with being the first black president—or first black anything for that matter. President Obama realized there would be some black people in America with false hopes. People who thought that some-how overnight the racial economic gap would close, blacks would be equal to their white counterparts and all racial discrimination would magically disappear. I believe it was a direct message to these people saying, "Don't view me as a Savior! View me as a partner and join me in the movement." President Obama understands progress. He knows it would have been impossible for him to run for office, if not for the efforts of many courageous people that came before him.

Martin Luther King was in his early twenties when he became an activist for the Civil Rights Movement. He, along with countless others, helped bring about change in our society that created the platform we stand on today. Contrary to popular belief, the Civil Rights Movement is not over. We've been successful in many battles, but the war against racial inequality has not yet been won. There is yet more progress to be made.

Not everyone has to be the next Martin Luther King or Barack Obama. What about all the ordinary people who marched on Washington beside Dr. King or the millions of African Americans who helped vote President Obama into office? If we all just do our part that contribution will be enough. What we cannot do, under any circumstance, is work against the grain. The self-inflicted wounds and friendly fire must cease.

Our ancestors fought hard for the right to vote, yet we choose not to cast a ballot. They fought equally as hard to desegregate schools, yet we still choose to dropout. This phenomenon must change. We have to transcend this impoverished state of mind. We have to get back in school and start developing our future leaders. Just as our ancestors paved the way for us, we have to press forward and open new doors for the next generations.

2

MY STORY

"I did what I knew how to do, and when I knew better, I did better."
—Maya Angelou

Though I feel this chapter is the most irrelevant because this book is not about me, its purpose is necessary to qualify the content that surrounds it—not as fact, but as adequate support of my relationship to the subject matter. In other words, if you're looking for "street cred'," here it is…

My coming of age was no different than any other inner-city child living in urban poverty. Though our experiences may differ, we are alike in the sense that we all were exposed to the darker side of life at a very young age. Drugs, gangs, guns and prostitution were all a part of our everyday lives. Imagery most parents wouldn't allow their children to view on a movie screen, we watched first hand. We accepted this as being the norm and continued on our quest to adulthood, internalizing these images and them shaping our perspective along the way.

I was raised in the Richard Flower Homes, a low-income public housing project in Robbins, IL. Robbins (a.k.a. Mudville) is a small impoverished community on the southwest side of Chicago. Though Robbins is technically a suburb of Chicago, anyone who has ever driven through the area can attest to its inner-city feel; garbage in the street, liquor stores on every corner, abandoned buildings and various public housing quarters. This is true of several towns and villages on the southern outskirts of Chicago. Their high poverty and crime rates closely resemble that of the inner-city making them nothing more than an extension of it.

I lived in the projects for eighteen years until I left for college, but as a family we lived there for more than forty years before moving out in 2006. Mostly, I lived there with Mama, Granny, Auntie Joyce and my two older siblings, Dee and Nika. I say, "mostly" because over the years we had several family members come live with us for two to three years at a time.

At one point, there were eight people living in a three bedroom unit with only one bathroom (those of you who grew up in a similar household can sympathize with me). I shared a bedroom with my mother and both siblings, until finally Auntie Joyce moved out and Dee and I moved into her old room. I was seventeen years old at the time. I enjoyed my new room for less than a year, before moving off to college.

Life in the projects was fun as a young child. There was always something to do and someone to do it with. All the families lived within a two-block radius. Most households had at least three children, so making friends was a breeze. If one of your homeboys couldn't come out to play, because he was in trouble, there were at least five more kids you could hang out with. We did it all! We would play basketball on the courts, or freeze tag in the playground. We would skateboard through the alleys, or ride bikes until sundown. We would enjoy every moment of sunlight before it was gone and the street lights came on indicating it was time to go home. Then the next day, we would wake up and do the same thing all over again.

I knew that living in the projects meant we were poor because of the remarks I would hear people make, but I never considered my neighborhood dangerous. My siblings and I ran the streets without a care in the world. The only thing we were concerned with was having fun. Still, life in the projects did have its downsides. Living in such close proximity to other families created its share of issues. The hardest issue for me to overlook was the migration of roaches and rats from one home to the next. Since we lived in row houses and shared a wall with another family, if they lived in filth, inevitably their pests would become our pests.

Growing up, my family was considered "the rich of the poor." My mother had a job, we owned a car and we went grocery shopping regularly. We were also a part of the upper echelon of families that actually went on vacations in the summer. Most of the time, it was to Wisconsin Dells, or Six Flags, but when I was ten years old, Mama saved up enough money to take us to Disney World! Now that may sound like no big deal to some Americans, but when you live in the hood, taking a trip to Disney World is like flying to the moon. Most of my friends had never been outside the state of Illinois.

People always assumed we thought we were better than everyone else because we didn't associate much with other families. This was Granny's way of keeping down trouble. It seemed like every summer there was at least one family feud. It usually started with two families being close and then the next thing you know…the families were at war.

Our family was too small for feuds. Granny only had four children, of which, only two of them had children of their own: my mother and Aunt Angie (who lived across the street with her four daughters). We needed more testosterone. The only time I can remember us being the infamous "family feud of the summer" was when Auntie Joyce got punched in the face by a man two-times her size. I don't remember how the argument started, but the commotion drew both families out of the house. At that point all hell broke loose and the two families were in an all out brawl. We made it outside just in time to see Auntie Joyce fall to the ground. At one point I turned and saw my grandmother swinging her cane like she was chasing a Major League curveball. Luckily the police showed up before things escalated too far.

Growing up, I shied away from fighting. It wasn't until my mother bought me my first weight set, in the eighth grade, that I started thinking I was tough. My brother on the other hand was the complete opposite. I think he struggled with math because he never backed down from a fight, no matter how outnumbered he was. I probably would have considered him brave, if he was alone when it happened, but since I was usually there, I thought it was just plain stupid that he would get us both beat up. Mama always told us, "If one of you get in a fight, both of you betta' get in a fight." If we didn't, she would give whoever didn't help a whoopin' when we came home. One time, Dee and I were walking home from the store and he got into an argument with about six guys and I bailed on him. I figured if I left, I only had to face one person (my mother), rather than three, so I played the odds. In retrospect, I should've stayed and fought side-by-side with my brother, but we both responded instinctively. He was a natural-born fighter. I was a gifted sprinter.

My brother had a different father from Nika and me. Mama always said that Dee took after his father. They both struggled with anger management. Dee's father liked to drink and become violent. He would polish off a fifth or two, and then attempt to turn my mother into a human punching bag, so she left him. Shortly after, Dee's father moved away to another state and rarely ever came back around.

When Mama became pregnant with Dee, she was in her sophomore year of college at Southern Illinois University in Edwardsville. With no support system away at college, she chose to drop out of school and move back home to the projects. Right after my brother was born, my mother and father started dating. For all intents and purposes, he was dad to all of us, though none of us called him, "Dad"; we simply referred to him as "Sherman."

Sherman lived about five minutes away from us (on the other side of Robbins) with my paternal grandparents, Aunt Darlene and her son Torune. This area of Robbins was mostly single family homes. It was considered to be a step-up from the public housing my family lived in. Torune was never allowed to visit me. It was considered to be too dangerous. Whenever we wanted to hangout, I had to go over my grandparents' house. If my neighborhood was too dangerous for my cousin, I often wondered why Sherman never worked to put his children in a safer environment. Sherman worked off and on (more off than on) throughout my childhood; mainly, little odd jobs that paid under the table. It was just enough money for him to support himself.

Mama was the primary breadwinner of our two-roof family. She was usually at work most of the day. She came home just in time to cook (if Granny hadn't already) and start getting ready for work the next day. It felt like all she ever did was work and iron her clothes to get ready for work.

Mama took her job very seriously. She rarely ever missed a day of work. Throughout my childhood, she quit or was laid off from different jobs, but she never stayed unemployed for any length of time. In between jobs, she collected unemployment and used government welfare to make sure we had food on the table, but she never stopped looking for work in the process.

I referred to our family as "two-roof" because Sherman did not live with us, yet we did activities together just as a traditional family would. We would go grocery shopping or to the mall. On the weekends, we would go out to dinner or to the movies. Most of our time together was spent outside of the house.

Granny didn't care much for Sherman. In fact, she downright hated him and due to some events (arguments and fights) that had occurred in the past, Sherman was not allowed inside the house. Whenever he came to visit, he would stand outside and call-in through the window. Just the sound of Sherman's voice made the hairs on Granny's neck stand up. Shortly after Sherman came around, Granny usually began fussing and outwardly expressing her dislike for him. I loved my grandmother dearly. She was like my second mother, but when she would start belittling my father, I would get upset and we would usually end up in an argument.

"Torri! Yo' no good daddy is at the door for you!"

"Why he gotta be all that?"

"Because he is!"

"Ok. But didn't you just say that the other day when he came over? You sound like a broken record."

"You only gettin' mad because that's your daddy and all you think about is daddy, daddy, daddy! You want everybody else to think about daddy, daddy, daddy!"

"That is all you think about. He ain't said nothin' and you already fussin'. He must stay on your mind day and night. Ha!"

"Honey please! I got much mo' important things to think about than his a$$. I wish I had a gun. I would just shoot him, so I don't have to deal with the a$$hole no mo'!" (Getting up from her rocker and walking into the kitchen)

"Ok Granny. I'll buy you one tomorrow. Bye!"

(Exiting the house)

As a child, I loved my dad and I looked up to him. Sherman was the first person to introduce me to working out. I can remember not being strong enough to do a push-up, so he would put me on his back while he did them. Perched on his back as he went up and down I thought to myself, "My daddy's da' strongest daddy in da' world!"

My dad also started my love for old school music. He would play the O'jays, Marvin Gaye, Teddy Pendergrass and his favorite, Sam Cooke. We would stand around dancing and singing for hours. To this day, I still prefer to listen to old school over most other genres of music.

Every once in awhile Sherman and I would watch *Jeopardy* together and it never ceased to amaze me how much trivial information he had stored away in his brain. He would often sit around the house reading encyclopedias for fun. At the time I thought it was boring, but as I got older, I started to develop this habit of reading dictionaries (I attribute that to my dad and his thirst for knowledge).

When he had the time, Sherman was a pretty good parent. The problem was that most of his time was spent elsewhere. For as far back as I can remember, my dad has been addicted to crack cocaine and because of his addiction, he would pick and choose when he wanted to be a father. I would always joke with him and say, "You love your white child (cocaine) more than me!"

Initially, Sherman started off as a drug dealer, but he could not withstand the temptation and curiosity eventually got the best of him. As a result of his addiction, he could never work a regular job. Not because he couldn't pass the drug test (he would have me provide a urine sample for him prior to the test), but because he would disappear for days unexcused resulting in termination.

For many years he worked off-and-on for a family-owned moving company. The owner, Vinny, was an older white man with an extremely bad temper. Vinny was also very cheap. There was usually only a 3-4 man crew (including the owner). The crew consisted of family members and lower-class labor that he could pay under-the-table. My dad was the latter. Depending on the size of the move and distance to the new location, they would try to do 2-3 jobs in one day. A few times they were undermanned and I tagged along to help, but that was short lived. At the time I was about eight or nine, just strong enough to lift a few boxes. Sherman and the rest of the crew shouldered the heavy stuff.

One day while we were at a job, my dad and Vinny were coming down the stairs with a large piece of furniture. Vinny was giving instructions to my dad as he backed down the stairs. All of a sudden, Sherman took a false step and the furniture hit up against the wall leaving a small hole. Vinny lost it! I've never seen someone so infuriated.

"You stupid son of a b*t@$! You Muthaf*^k@*! You Dumb F*%#!"

I stood there as Vinny went on a two-minute rant, threatening and degrading my dad in every way possible. I watched Sherman stand there and not say a word.

It was an honest mistake, I thought. I could not believe my dad would let someone disrespect him in such a way. I could feel the hairs on my neck standing up as Vinny continued hurling insults. He could care less that I was present. He viewed Sherman as some dumb junky he hired who couldn't follow directions and I was just the junky's son.

When we finished up for the day, we left and I swore on my life that I would never work for that man again. I kept my word and never returned, but my dad continued working for Vinny for several years. That day I learned that there is something worth more than money... dignity!

As I started to come of age, I began to see my pops in a different light. I would see the young dope boys in the community sell him crack. I would hear rumors in school about him getting beat up over something drug related. Over time this turned me bitter towards Sherman. All the love and admiration I once had for him turned into disgust and resentment. The man I once viewed as, "the strongest daddy in da' world" was now too weak to defend himself against the young dope boys in the community.

I also started to view my entire neighborhood in a different light. The place I used to feel safe to roam had now become a war zone. Gang activity had picked up and drive-by shootings were becoming more and more common. Now, if you were playing outside you had to make sure you were alert. If you heard anything that sounded like gunshots, you had to be ready to hit the ground.

Eight years old, outside one evening with my sister catching lightning bugs, a car came flying down the street. The driver must have been going about 70 mph. This stood out because my complex had speed bumps in the street about 20 meters apart, so only a drunk or someone who was up to no good would be driving that fast. We ignored it and continued to chase lightning bugs. All of a sudden, the same car came down the street again. This time, they were going about 80 mph. They flew right past us. When they reached the other end of the street, they started unloading round after round with semi-automatic weapons.

Sherman ran and grabbed Nika and me. He tucked us under each arm and bolted into the house (under these extreme circumstances he was allowed to take refuge inside the house). Everybody stretched flat on the floor. Stop, drop, and get flat were the standard procedures when we heard gun shots—our ghetto fire(arm) drill. I can remember thinking sometimes, "Man…do we gotta' get on da' flo', errtime' we hear gunshots?" This night was a little different than the others. The shooting continued longer than usual. Every police officer in Robbins (and neighboring towns) was called to the scene. Finally, after about two hours all the shooting and sirens ceased.

Later that night, we found out that a ten year old boy, Mikey, was killed by a stray bullet that went through his window. Even though I didn't know Mikey, after hearing the news of his death, I was devastated. I knew of other people who had been killed, but never someone so close to my age. For the next couple of weeks I was afraid to go outside, in fear that I could end up like Mikey.

There were numerous arrests that followed the shooting. Some people were sentenced to more than twenty-five years in prison. The streets were hot. The police took over the entire projects. They made any groups standing on the corners disperse, which cut down on the gang activity. They started to patrol more often, making it hard for the dope boys to make money, so the drug trade dried up. The neighborhood was as safe as it had ever been.

A few years passed and then everything went back to the way it was. Except now, I was a little bit older, so gangs became more of a problem. It wasn't an issue of more gang violence; it was the pressure to join a gang that picked up. Where I lived, everybody was Gangster Disciples (a.k.a. GD), so if you chose to join a gang, you only had one choice (unless you wanted to get jumped every time you walked outside of the house). Since there was no other gang in my projects, even if you weren't GD, everybody usually acted like they were. We greeted each other by saying, "What up Folk?" Folk referred to the FOLK Nation—an alliance of gangs represented under the six-point star, which includes the Gangster Disciples.

When we shook hands, we would "shake up." Shakin' up refers to a special handshake reserved only for fellow gang members. If you wore a hat, it was to the right and more than likely, it was blue or black. If you wanted to prove that you weren't telling a lie you would pound both fists together—one on top of the other—and "stack it on the Boss" or "put it on Larry Hoover" (one of the founding fathers of the GDs). The whole projects took on the identity of the GDs. I can't speak for the rest of the projects, but I only did it because that was the culture. I had no desire to be a Gangster Disciple.

Even though I was too young to join the real gang, they started a group called the "Shorty Gs." The Shorty Gs were a group of kids, who were too young to be jumped into the gang, so they were like Gangster Disciples in-training. They learned all the literature and governing rules of the Gangster Disciples, and once they reached a certain age they were officially jumped into the gang.

They tried to recruit me to become a Shorty G, but I refused. My mother had always warned me never to join a gang. Plus, I knew that the Shorty Gs engaged in criminal activity, which I didn't want to be associated with. Most of the SGs' parents were either on drugs or in jail. The elder gang members used the SGs to do their dirty work. They would have the SGs hold their drugs, knowing that if they got caught they would only be prosecuted as juveniles. They would have SG's break into cars and steal radios, speakers, etc. If they could convince them to do it, they would even have the SGs shoot rival gang members. They took total advantage of the SGs innocence and used their youthful enthusiasm for personal gain (just like the warlords who brainwash child soldiers in Africa).

When I refused to join the group, the elder gang members ordered the Shorty Gs to jump me. These were all kids that I went to school with, so they gave me one last chance during class to join the group. I declined. After school, they were waiting for me. I peeked out of one of the exits and saw five SGs standing outside, so I walked around to the other side of the building and exited out of those doors. I started walking, until I heard someone yell, "There he go!" as they came chasing after me. I had at least a thirty-yard head start, so there was no way any of them were catching me.

I made it home and ran in the door gasping for air. Mama walked over to me and asked, "What's wrong?" so I explained the situation. I knew I wasn't supposed to ever run from a bully but "This was different," I thought. I was outnumbered by four people, but that didn't matter to my mother. She grabbed me by the collar and walked out the door. By this time the SGs had caught up to me and were standing outside my house. Mama motioned to them, "Which one of you wanna' fight my son?"

Nobody said a word or moved a muscle.

"Who eva' wanna fight my son, come fight him right now?" she said boldly. Again, nobody moved.

My mother grabbed me and started walking back into the house and said, "If you're too scared to fight him one on one, then leave him alone."

As we walked into the house, one of the guys yelled, "We'll see you tomorrow!"

Initially, I was mad at my mother for making me go back outside, but after witnessing what happened, I understood her reasoning and I was glad she made me do it. The next day I got into an altercation with the same dudes, only this time I didn't run. Two SGs jumped me, but I held my ground until a teacher came and broke up the fight. I never had a problem with the Shorty Gs again. They knew I wasn't scared anymore. It also didn't hurt that I had an older brother who was willing to take on an entire army by himself.

The older I became, I was able to see first-hand what the GDs were all about and I wanted nothing to do with them, so moving forward I gave everyone a normal handshake. I wore my hats straight. The phrase, "What up Folk?" became foreign to me. I stopped embracing all aspects of their tradition. I joined the park district baseball and football team and began learning how to play organized sports; so most of my evenings were spent at practice instead of in the streets.

This was also at the point when Mama decided she was tired of dealing with Sherman and his constant drug abuse. For over a decade, she had been listening to the same lie about how he was going to get clean and turn his life around. He was showing no signs of stopping and his drug addiction was escalating to the point where that he began stealing from his family. Nothing was safe around him. When I came to visit, he would give me money and steal it back in the middle of the night. I started hiding the money somewhere around the bedroom, but he would find it every time. I tried to outsmart him by hiding the money in my socks and sleeping with them on. That way, he would have to touch me in order to get the money out and hopefully I would wake up. In theory, it should have worked. Come morning I would wake up with my socks on and the money would be gone.

One summer, my grandparents went out of town for a family reunion and Sherman was left home alone. At the time, the house was being remodeled, so along with everything else in the house there were rolls of carpet, tiling and brand new chandeliers in the living room. When my grandparents returned home from their trip, they walked into an empty house. Nothing was left. Sherman had stolen everything including the chandeliers and he was nowhere to be found.

Realizing Sherman was making little effort to get clean, thus marriage was out of the question, Mama broke off the relationship. She started dating George—a gentleman she met through a co-worker. George loved to party, so he would often take Mama out for a night on the town. He was fun and a refreshing change from Sherman, who never wanted to go anywhere or do anything. Mama grew very fond of George, so much so that when I was twelve she sat me and my siblings down and told us, "I'm moving out." She had been a mother since she was twenty-one years old. She never had the chance to be young and have fun. Her life for the past fourteen years revolved around work and her kids. She was tired. For the first time in many years, she was enjoying her youth, so she decided to put herself first. My siblings seemed to have embraced the idea rather positively, but I was heartbroken. Her decision would put a strain on our relationship for years to come.

With Mama gone, Granny became our primary caregiver. She

tried her best to keep us in line, but at her age Granny didn't have the energy to keep up with us. As a result, there was a fundamental shift in my behavioral patterns. I started hanging out with my older brother and his friends. They were only a few years older than me, but they had already begun drinking and smoking weed. None of us were old enough to buy alcohol, so we would pick one of the many drunks standing around the liquor store and give him a couple dollars to pay for our liquor. There were at least one or two of Dee's friends, who experimented with selling weed (equivalent to sticks and seeds) so we always had a supply, but if we wanted the "good stuff," we had to purchase it from the dope boys on the block. We would stay out all night drinking hard liquor and smoking blunt after blunt in my middle school's playground.

It was always fun to see how stupid everybody would act once we all were high and intoxicated, but I never enjoyed the actual drinking and smoking part. Smoking always made my saliva thicken, so I would have this irritating gagging feeling and the liquor just made me down right sick! None of us had jobs, so it wasn't like we were purchasing top-shelf liquor. The cheap alcohol we were drinking probably would have peeled paint off of a car.

We would sometimes invite girls to join us in the playground. There seemed to always be three of us for every one of them. We would all drink and get high, then engage in mischief that need not be repeated. After feeling like my mother had turned her back on me for another man and seeing the way these young girls disrespected themselves, I practically lost all respect for women.

Growing up, I always heard older guys talk about women as if they were all money-hungry sluts, but I never bought into that theory. Largely, because I was raised by women and the close relationship I had with my mother. Now that she was gone, I started to question my beliefs. I knew no matter how strong George's feelings were for my mother, they paled in comparison to my love for her...so "Why would she leave me?"

My mother was the first woman to ever break my heart. As her youngest child, I knew we had formed a very special bond. To others, Mama was probably just some poor young black girl living in the projects with her three kids, but to me she was the Queen of the Nile. I adored her. Part of the reason why my relationship with my pops started to deteriorate was because of the way that he treated her. It killed me to see my mother unhappy. Whenever she was down, I always tried to lift her spirits (I remember, as a child, wishing that I was my mother's companion, so I could treat her the way she deserved to be treated.)

When another man came along and broke our bond, the pain I felt turned me bitter. I found myself growing disrespectful towards women. Not grossly disrespectful, but there was a noticeable change in my attitude towards the opposite sex. It went from one of admiration to one of disdain. I started embracing the words of the older guys in the hood. They introduced me to "the game" and gave me my first lessons on how to treat a woman. The game had many rules, but the underlying theme was that, "all women are whores to be used at your disposal." The more educated I became on "the game" the more I pursued the opposite sex. This would ultimately lead to my first sexual encounter. So at the promising age of twelve, not only was I drinking and smoking, I was now sexually active.

My drug and alcohol phase lasted a little over a year until my mother made the decision to come back home. She sensed that her children were getting out of control and her role as disciplinarian had been challenged. Also, hanging out with Dee and his friends was starting to put a strain on the relationship between me and my best friend, Travis. Travis wasn't into drinking or smoking, so every time we were about to start, he would leave. One night, we all went to the playground to get high. When we got there I decided I didn't want to smoke that night, so I left. I never went back.

When Mama returned home, Sherman started doing everything in his power to create turmoil in her new relationship. He would come to her job and pick fights with George in the parking lot—as George waited to meet her after work. He would follow them around the city to nightclubs and cause scenes in the parking lots. George was extremely timid, so all the harassment was starting to take its toll on him and their relationship. Mama eventually filed for an order of protection, but even that didn't stop the harassment. Sherman continued to stalk them and when the police showed up, he would flee.

One Friday, Mama was driving home from work and a car came up from behind and started to ram her, as if they were trying to run her off the road. She looked in her rearview mirror and saw that it was Sherman. I believe it was at that exact moment when she decided that she was fed up. Mama would often come home looking tired from a long day at work, but that day she walked in the door with a look of determination on her face. I knew something was wrong before she ever said a word.

"Mama what's wrong?" Nika asked,.

"Nothin'…I'm just so sick and tired of ya'll father. He gone make me do somethin' very bad to him."

She began telling the story of her frightful drive home from work. I sat quietly as Granny and Nika listened and encouraged her to go to the police, but Mama was tired of going to the police and watching them do nothing. She was ready to take matters into her own hands. If Sherman would have showed up at the house that evening, I'm convinced that would have been the end of his days on this earth.

A few days passed (as well as my 14th birthday) and everything went back to normal. Mama seemed to be in good spirits. I was excited because I was two days away from my first high school football practice. Sherman had promised to take me shopping for new cleats as a belated birthday present. There was a fifty-fifty chance that he would show, but I had a good feeling about this one. Shortly before the noon hour, my pops pulled up in front of the house. I was so excited I ran outside to meet him. He walked up the sidewalk and started to yell inside.

"Pooh-Pooh! What you doin' in there?" (Pooh-Pooh was my father's pet name for my mother). Mama did not respond.

Knowing what had transpired just a few days ago, I suggested that he wait for me in the car while I put on some clothes to avoid any conflict. He agreed. I quickly walked back into the house and found Mama in the kitchen boiling water.

"What are you doing?" I asked innocently.

"Making some spaghetti" she replied.

"Ok...well I gotta go, Sherman 'sposed to buy me some new cleats. I gotta hurry up and get dressed before he changes his mind." I ran up the stairs to the bathroom and closed the door.

As I was getting ready, I could hear muffled sounds coming from downstairs and then all of a sudden the noise stopped. The next sound I heard was Nika's voice calling Sherman to the front door.

"Sherman...Sherman, come here for a second!"

There was a long pause followed by a loud scream. It startled me for a second. In that same moment, my mind started to put two and two together. I had a flashback of my mother boiling water in the kitchen. Before I opened the door, I already knew what had happened. At this point, I could hear Mama yelling out the front door.

"I told yo' a$$ to leave me alone!"

I opened the bathroom door, ran down the stairs and pushed past my mother and sister to get outside. Sherman was lying on the ground soaking wet and shaking. My mother had thrown boiling hot water through the screen door onto him.

I yelled out, "Somebody call the ambulance!" to the crowd of people beginning to form.

I ran over to him and tried to provide comfort. I put my arm around him and said, "The ambulance is on its way." I could see patches of loose skin start to run down his neck and back like sweat. I had never seen anything like this before in my life. I thought for sure he was going to die.

The paramedics arrived shortly after. They lifted Sherman onto a gurney and moved quickly towards the truck. I sat on the ground and cried, as I watched the paramedics hoist my father into the ambulance and the police stuff my mother into a squad car. Though both images were hard to bear, I could not help but wonder if Sherman was going to be ok. I quickly realized that underneath all my anger and resentment, I loved my pops.

Sherman had suffered second and third degree burns on 40% of his torso. He spent 3 weeks recovering in the burn unit of Loyola Hospital. After spending three nights in jail, Mama was released on I-bond until her court date. During our visits with Sherman in the hospital, Nika and I repeatedly begged him not to press charges against Mama. He couldn't find it in his heart to let her get away Scott free for her actions, but he didn't want to hurt his children by sending their mother to jail. During the hearing, the state's attorney asked Sherman if he was pursuing jail time (for my mother). He said, "No," but informed the attorney that he still wanted to press charges. Mama pleaded not guilty on grounds of self-defense. But after all the evidence was reviewed and witnesses interviewed, the court found her actions to be premeditated (e.g., boiling water, calling Sherman to the door). Mama was found guilty of domestic battery. She received a conditional discharge with a mandatory year of anger management classes. However, she never had any problems with Sherman, and his bullying, going forward. Once she satisfied the conditions of her discharge, Mama tried to move forward with her life and forget about what had happened. It took me years to forgive her for what she did.

Sports Euphoria

No matter what was going on in life, sports always provided me an escape. Whether it was baseball, football or basketball, for however long I played nothing else mattered. Baseball and basketball were fun, but I fell in love with football. Unlike the other two, football allowed me to take the pain I was feeling and inflict it on my opponent. I first played for the Robbins Eagles—the community park district team. On Sunday mornings everybody would stop what they were doing to come watch us play. The sidelines were filled with parents, family members, community leaders, business owners, police officers, high school coaches…even the dope boys would take a break to come watch.

Win or lose, after every game Mama would take me and my siblings out to eat and celebrate. My memories of the actual games are vague, but I can vividly remember running around the restaurant with my cleats and dirty football pants on. Mama made it a point to be at every game, home and away, rain or shine. My siblings and other family members would usually accompany her. Football became the centerpiece of our family.

The game of football came easy to me. Playing running back highlighted many of my natural abilities. I had a knack for making people miss and finding seams in defenses. Plus I had pretty good speed, so I would make one defender miss and outrun everyone else. My nickname in the hood became "lil' NFL." It was ironic to witness how the dynamics changed once I became known around the hood as a football player. Nobody messed with me anymore. In fact, the hood rallied behind me. The same guys who tried to get me to sell dope, or jump me for not joining their gang started saying, "I bet not catch you out here on da' block!" They realized that I had the potential to do something greater with my life than sell drugs. Some of them had similar potential and watched their dreams slip away. They were now living the life of a dream deferred.

Though I never wanted to sell drugs, walking home from school my best friend Travis and I were often approached by crack addicts looking for dope. If we wanted to go down that route, it would have been easy to do. The drugs sold themselves. We just had to be willing to deal with the consequences, if we were caught. The fear of being caught never discouraged me, because like most young people I thought I was smarter than everyone else. It was my own father's addiction that made me hate drugs and everybody that had anything to do with them.

I did my best to stay out of the streets and in the books, in hopes that one day all my hard work would carry me out of the projects. Throughout my school years, I was a pretty good student. I always took pride in my assignments. Like sports, I saw it as a competition and I never wanted to lose. Whenever test time came around it was "game time." My favorite part of it all was the next day in class when the teacher would pass out the results. Usually the top three scores were announced first and the students' names read aloud. The teacher would say, "...and our top score was a 100% with a perfect 30 out of 30 by...Torri Stuckey." I would walk up very nonchalantly and get my test. Deep inside, I relished the moment. Of course I was not the top scorer every time, but I was usually in the top three.

By the time I reached high school, my yearning for knowledge turned into a lust for the opposite sex. Straight A's and spelling bees no longer interested me. As I began high school, I was placed into all core honors classes. When I walked into my Honors Biology class the first day, I was one of only three black students in the class. This was in extreme contrast with my middle school, which was predominately African American. That day I went home and started working on my mother. I convinced her that the material was too tough and that I needed to drop down to regular classes. Mama saw honors classes as icing on the cake; all she really cared about was that I brought home good grades. After a week of torture, she gave me permission to change my classes. I dropped all my honors classes, except for Algebra. The next day, I joined all my homeboys and other people from the hood down in the regular classes.

Regular classes were so easy that I rarely brought homework home. I would sit in the back of class while the teacher was lecturing and do the homework assignment. By this time, we were on the fourth day of the same lecture, so I wasn't missing out on anything. When it came time for tests, we would go over the information all week and take the test on Friday. Usually on Friday the teacher would come in and say,

"I don't think everyone is prepared to take this test, so we will take it on Monday." Due to the weekend, we would use Monday as a review day and finally take the test on Tuesday. After almost two weeks on the same topic, I could just about take the test blindfolded, so I focused most of my attention on football and the ladies.

That same year, I was moved up a level to play for the sophomore football team. I earned the starting running back spot. That season we went a perfect 9-0, beating our arch rival for the first time in many years. I set a new school record for most rushing yards in a season. The previous record had been in place for more than a decade.

The next season I moved up to the varsity level. We continued to have success as a team and I started to become a household name, not only in my neighborhood, but all throughout the Chicago area. I started receiving letters from different colleges and universities. By the time I reached the twelfth grade, I was one of the top running backs in the state and I was nationally ranked. I was recruited by over fifty schools and had more than twenty scholarship offers.

Every week during my senior year, dozens and dozens of letters poured in from schools all across the country. Coaches would come to my school often and I would be pulled out of class, so I could "randomly" bump into them in the hallway. This all happened before coaches could legally contact me directly. Once the time came when coaches could contact me, I went from enjoying the attention to wishing everything was over. At night, I had to set a window of time in which I would accept phone calls from coaches; otherwise, the phone would ring all throughout the evening making it difficult to prepare for school the next day. To cut down on some of the interaction, I narrowed my choices down to five universities—Northwestern being my top choice. Once Northwestern realized they had a strong chance of signing me, the head coach decided to come out for a home visit.

It was a cold winter night in December 1999. Mama was in the kitchen preparing dinner, while I was in the living room playing lookout. Both the coaches from Northwestern were white. The only time white people drove through my complex was if they wanted drugs, so I was a little concerned about how their arrival would play out. Once it got closer to the time they were supposed to arrive, I started periodically looking out of the window. It was about my fourth time checking when I saw a white SUV sitting in the middle of the street. I figured it must be them, so I grabbed my coat and headed outside to greet them. Before I could get my foot out the door, a couple dope boys were already en route to the car in full sprint. I started yelling, "No... No! No! No!" but they did not hear me. By the time I reached the car they already had nickel and dime bags out at the window. Between me yelling and the frightened look on the coaches' faces, they finally got the picture and walked off. Despite that initial awkward incident, Northwestern's scholarship offer was still on the table. I accepted.

The NU World

As a youth, I would often hear the words African Americans and minorities used interchangeably. I understood the definition of a minority and I rationalized that relative to the U.S. population African Americans were a smaller number, but I never really understood what it meant to be a minority. Growing up in an all-black community, where I was surrounded by black families on every corner, the word "minority" meant absolutely nothing to me. That would change.

Attending high school outside of my community had introduced me to a more diverse culture. There were Caucasian students and a large number of Hispanics, so I was even exposed to a different language; but there were still enough of my people from the hood at the high school that I was able to stay in my comfort zone. It wasn't until I graduated and accepted an athletic scholarship to Northwestern University that my true understanding of the word "minority" started to take form.

After signing my letter of intent to attend Northwestern University, I remember receiving a random phone call from a young woman. She was a graduate student in Northwestern's School of Education. She wanted to interview me about my decision to attend Northwestern. I agreed without any thought as to why I was chosen to be interviewed. As she began to ask questions, I realized this was not a random call. She had done her research and found out that I was from a small impoverished community on the south side of Chicago. She wanted to know if I felt like I was at a disadvantage coming from a public school, or if I was at all nervous about fitting in, since most of the students I would be attending college with had attended private schools and were from middle to upper-middle class neighborhoods? At the time, I just brushed it off as some graduate student with too much time on her hands. I gave her a couple quick answers and went on about my business. Little did I know that interview was foreshadowing what would soon be my reality.

Though it was only about an hour drive north from the south side of Chicago to Northwestern's campus, it was indeed a new world. The entire culture changed. I moved from a culture that celebrated toughness to one that celebrated intelligence. No one cared if you could fight or what gang you represented. Those matters were looked at as juvenile and unscholarly.

I can remember arriving to campus for the first time. It was a beautiful summer day. There were people outside jogging along the lake, walking their dogs and riding their bicycles. The sound of birds chirping filled the air, as we wound up and down the tree-lined roads past the manicured lawns and million dollar homes. It was very quiet and peaceful, I thought, "Wow! This place is…different."

To be honest, I was a little drawn back at first, because in the hood if you were running down the street it was because the police were after you, somebody was chasing you, or you were racing to a customer's car, but no one ran around the neighborhood for fun or exercise. "So this is how rich people live" I said, as I continued to inhale my new surroundings. I had never encountered this kind of wealth. The atmosphere was polar opposite of anything I had ever experienced. Everyone looked happy. It felt as though no one had a care in the world.

As we parked and headed towards the dorms, I crossed paths with another black student.

"Hey, how's it going?" he smiled and said very properly.

I wasn't quite sure how to respond to him, because where I was from black people didn't speak to each other in such a manner. He sounded like a "white boy." I gathered myself and replied, "What up?"

I knew the transition from the streets of Robbins to the halls of Northwestern would be a struggle. I expected most of the student body to be spoiled rich kids, who I had little to nothing in common with, but I always took comfort in the fact that I would have my teammates. Though I didn't know most of them, "football players are the same everywhere"…so I thought. I figured most guys were like me and passed through admissions by the skin of their teeth and were only here because they received a scholarship; otherwise, they could not afford the tuition.

In reality, I was surrounded by brilliant minds, guys who scored nearly perfect 36s and 1600s on their ACT and SAT exams. Their athletic ability paled in comparison to their scholastic gifts. While I had never thought of doing anything other than playing in the NFL after college, their plans were to become successful doctors, lawyers and engineers. Most of my teammates came from middle to upper-middle class backgrounds. These were the sons of top bank executives, surgeons, former professional athletes, sports agents and TV broadcasters. The stadium parking lot was full of luxury cars (Lexus, Audi, Infiniti, Cadillac, etc.) yet none belonged to the coaching staff.

There were a few guys from the hood like me, but we were the minority. Unlike high school, there weren't enough of us for me to stay in my comfort zone. As a team, most of our time was spent together at the stadium, so I was forced to interact with teammates from various backgrounds. For the most part, everyone got along, but even those who disliked each other put aside their differences for the greater good of the team. The locker room became our sanctuary. It was an open forum for discussion of any and all topics. Some people shared more information than necessary; others did not share any at all. I typically just listened to what everyone else had to say. There was plenty of useless and trivial information shared, but I also learned a great deal.

Something I picked up on early from our discussions is that most of my black teammates had white girlfriends and most of the ones who were single preferred dating white girls. I found that very alarming. "Do these guys wanna be white?" I thought. I was determined to find out.

I remember one of my black teammates showing me a photo album from his prom. There must have been over a hundred pictures and as I flipped through, I never saw one other African American besides him. From his date to all the other couples, he was the only African American, but that didn't seem to bother him one bit. In every picture he smiled full of glee and gave "thumbs up" with the rest of his Caucasian comrades.

"Did you ever feel like an outcast?" I asked.

"What do you mean?" he said with a puzzled look on his face.

I could see in his eyes that he was being sincere. He honestly did not realize I was referring to his race, so I left it alone. His initial response was all the answer I needed.

I had another black teammate explain to me that he only dates white girls. As shocking as that declaration was, his justification was even more outrageous. He further explained that he only dates white girls because, "black girls stink." Obviously, there were some deeper self-hatred issues going on here, but on the surface, he explained that most of the black girls he had come in contact with had a funny odor. Due to this fact, he has always dated outside of his race. With that being said, I had to ask the million dollar question.

"Your mother is black, does she stink?"

"MY MAMA DON'T STINK!" He emphatically replied.

As I continued to probe he began to recant his story by stating that he would date a black girl (that didn't stink), but would not go out of his way to meet her.

"Put it like this," he said, "If I was walkin' down the street and saw a bad black girl walkin' on the other side of the street, I wouldn't cross the street to holla at her, but if that was a bad a$$ white girl, I'm dodging cars and weaving thru traffic...you know what I mean?"

Unlike the other black teammate, this young man had not been raised in a predominately white neighborhood, or come from a highly privileged background. His family was a part of the regular working class like mine, only he was from the rural south. If anything, I expected these types of racial remarks to come from one of my white teammates who may not have interacted with many African Americans prior to college. Never did I imagine that I would hear these words of ignorance uttered from another African American.

After about a month of college I was convinced that I was going to stop dating black girls too. Not because they stunk or anything of that nature, but because the black girls on campus were so different from the ones back home. They all seemed uptight and conceited. They dressed boring; but the thing that turned me off the most was the way they talked. Most of them "talked white." I was used to sistas who utilized a little more slang when speaking, but these black girls talked proper. They seemed out of touch with the black culture. Their actual words themselves did not bother me. It was the idea that they were talking that way in the attempt to sound white that turned me off.

On the other hand, there was a certain level of gullibility and innocence that was reflected in their sound. Their lack of slang suggested they were ignorant to "the game," and I planned to take full advantage. I started hanging out with several girls, but no one girl in particular. I just enjoyed the presence of beautiful young ladies. With coed dorms, there were so many girls in such close proximity. My suite was right across the hall from a group of girls. No one ever told me about this element of college, or I probably would have tried to graduate high school early. It was enough to make people go crazy and that is exactly what some people did.

College is one of the few places where people can reinvent themselves. Everyone's background is a mystery, so strippers can become nuns and nice guys can become thugs and vice versa. It is where teenagers go to declare their independence from their parents. Some did it constructively and exerted themselves in school, while others liberated themselves by drinking and getting high, or partying and sleeping around with random people. I had been independent since I was twelve, so none of this "new found freedom" changed anything about my personality. I reflected back to the phone conversation I had with the graduate student and thought to myself, "I'm not at a disadvantage. If anything, growing up in the hood put me at an advantage." It prepared me for the darker side of college life. Partying and getting high was nothing new to me, but after my experimental phase, at twelve, I realized that drugs and alcohol was not conducive to what I was trying to accomplish on the football field.

My only bad habit was that I loved the ladies, so it was hard to give school and football my undivided attention. I was too busy trying to spit game at the ladies, but most of my time was spent repeating myself. There was an obvious language barrier. They struggled to understand my slang and I struggled to understand their idioms.

Throughout my first year of college the language barrier continued to present problems, even on the football field. One day during practice we were working on special teams and getting ready for a big game against the University of Wisconsin. We had just finished with kickoff and kickoff return and we were now practicing our punt coverage. As a freshman, I started on all special teams. On the punt team, I was the "gunner." The gunner is the person that stands out wide and runs down as fast as he can to make the tackle on the punt returner. I was a little gassed from the previous special teams and I guess I was not running down as fast as the head coach would have liked, so he called me out.

"Again! We're going to keep doing this until Torri Stuckey figures out this isn't high school anymore!" he shouted.

As a freshman, the two mistakes you try desperately to avoid are getting called out by a coach or making your teammates suffer for your actions. I tried my best to pick up my effort, but to no avail. We must have run through our punt coverage another 3 or 4 times, until finally the coach stopped play and called me over to him.

"What is your problem? Do you want to play?" he shouted.

"Yeah." I replied.

"Well then get you're a$$ down the field like it. Do you understand me?"

"Yeah!"

"Do you understand me?"

"Yeah!"

"Don't f*%#ing yeah me. I'm not one of your homeboys. Get the f%@# off the field." I was replaced by another freshman and practice continued.

As I stood on the sideline confused and wondering what I said wrong, I started to replay the conversation in my mind. Then it hit me, "he wanted me to say, 'Yes'." At first I felt a little foolish that I didn't pick up on his vibe, but the more I thought about it I started to get angry. I felt like he was picking on me. He knew I meant no disrespect by my response, that's just the way I talked. When he came to the south side of Chicago to offer me a scholarship, I likely accepted by saying, "yeah," so why was it a problem now? The longer I stood on the sideline the more enraged I became. Finally, I was allowed to get back on the field, as we ran through kickoff one more time. Once the ball was kicked, I ran down like a raging bull and I exploded into the returner causing a fumble and leaving my teammate on his back. The sideline went crazy!

As I jogged off the field, my coach called me over again. "That's the kind of effort I want to see from you every time. Make that the last time I have to force you to give me your best effort."

I shook my head in disagreement and said, "With all due respect, coach, that's bulls**t!"

"Excuse me!"

"If you don't like the way I talk, stop recruitin' on the south side of Chicago. You asked me a question and I answered you by saying 'Yeah.' That's the way I talk. When my mother asks me a question, I respond to her the same way. So the day you become more important to me than my own mother, then I'll say 'Yes' to you."

Had I known this was just the tip of the iceberg and that our relationship would continue to deteriorate over the next four years, I would have cut my losses right then and transferred to another school; but because I chose to attend Northwestern for reasons far beyond athletics, I decided to stay.

Football practice was tough, but adjusting to the college classroom presented an even greater task. When I walked into class, I would sometimes have flashbacks of my honors classes back in high school where there were also very few minority students. We covered a tremendous amount of material in a very short period of time. It felt like I was drinking water from a fire hydrant.

There were topics the professor would reference like they were common knowledge, yet I had no clue. After my first quarter of college, I was placed on academic probation. Not because the work was too hard, but because I had convinced myself I could not do it. I was overwhelmed by how much "smarter" everyone appeared. The professor would say, "If you have any questions please stop me," but I didn't want to be the only idiot that raised his hand. I felt everyone in class already looked at me as an athlete or some affirmative action recipient.

Unlike high school, Northwestern was on a trimester system, so just about every three months you started new classes. The upside was if you did not like a particular class, you would be done with it in less than three months. The downside was that you had to take midterms and finals three times a year. The trimesters moved very quickly. Two weeks into class professors began prepping for midterms. Playing as a true freshman meant that I would be traveling with the team for away games. This caused me to miss classes and play catch-up when I returned. Because of our rigorous schedule, we were allowed to take one less class during the season, but that only handicapped us. The off-season was just as demanding (minus the travel) with one more class added to the schedule.

Due to the stresses of school and an extremely hectic athletic commitment, I developed an ulcer. I had heard of it before, but I thought it was only something that elderly people suffered from. The doctor explained that ulcers are stress related and though common with elderly people they can develop at any age.

When the word got back to the coaches that I had an ulcer, I received an interesting phone call from my position coach.

"T-Stuck, I hear you have an ulcer, but I don't understand why. I've had ulcers before in the past. They are normally caused by stress and it's not like you come from a background with a maid and a butler. I'm sure coming from where you grew up that you've dealt with things far more stressful than this."

I didn't say a word, but I thought to myself, "Wow! That has to be the dumbest thing I have ever heard anybody say…EVER!" To think that because I grew up in the hood, I was immune to problems at school was ridiculous. The hood was my home, my safe haven; college represented uncharted territory.

Regardless of what happened at school, if I ever needed to be around "my people" home was only a train ride away. I took comfort in that fact. Going home was always a refreshing experience, but it was also a reminder that my family was still impoverished. It might sound crazy, but sometimes I felt guilty when I came back home. I was up at school living the good life; eating clam chowder and having philosophical debates over lunch, while my family was back home still dealing with life in the projects. It felt like I had moved out and left them behind. Part of me wanted to go back home and struggle with them until we all could make it out, but I knew staying the course offered me the best chance to make a change in our family situation. Unlike some athletes' relatives, my family never put pressure on me to be the savior of our family, but they never had to. The fact that my grandmother, who was in her seventies, had been living in poverty her entire life was motivation enough.

I did the train ride back and forth throughout my first year until I met a young lady and started dating her. Her name was Tay. She fell into the same category as the rest of the black girls in regards to the way she carried herself and her proper English; but there was something about her I found intriguing. Unlike the other girls I was hanging out with, it wasn't all about the physical with her. I wanted to know more about the person. Maybe it was because on the surface we seemed so different, but after letting go of a lot my personal biases and preconceived notions, we actually had a lot in common.

The more we talked; I realized she wasn't "stuck up." Tay was just raised by different standards than the girls I was used to entertaining. Her parents weren't filthy rich philanthropists who played around on the golf course all day. They were middle-class workers who had worked their way up from humble beginnings and tried very hard to provide their children with a better life. This was no different than all the long hours and hard work my mother had put in to provide my siblings and me with a stable childhood.

Another major issue I had with some of the other black students on campus was that I thought they had it "too easy" growing up. I despised them, because they didn't have to experience some of the hardships of my childhood. They walked around campus smiling as if life had been presented to them sunny side up, but that was not the case with this young lady. In fact, in her short lifetime, Tay had already experienced some deep tragedy. At seven years of age she lost her older sister to cancer.

Shortly after we started dating, I decided to bring Tay home to meet the family. This was a huge step. Up until this point, I had never brought a girl home to meet my mother. I was a little anxious to see how Mama and the rest of the family would receive her. I was afraid some people in the family might not be able to look deeper than the surface to embrace the inner person. I admittedly struggled with the superficial elements in the beginning, but over time I had the chance to get to know her and appreciate our differences. I wasn't too optimistic that the same could be accomplished in such a short visit home. Shockingly, overall she was a hit. The family loved her, but that didn't stop them from making little smart comments on the side about her proper English. It was harmless. I knew it was just their way of reacting to something unfamiliar.

The next year we came back home to visit for the holidays and my girlfriend was no longer the object of ridicule, I was. People started saying that I acted different. Family members started accusing me of talking different. I found myself stuck between a rock and a hard place. At school people thought I talked different and now back home people were saying that I acted different. I didn't speak well enough to meet Northwestern standards, but now I spoke too proper for "my people" back home. I was used to not fitting in at school, but I couldn't believe my own people were struggling to accept me. I let it bother me for about a day or so, and then I decided I was done trying to be who everyone else wanted me to be. I was just going to be Torri. Truthfully, I felt some aspects about me changing all along, but if the changes weren't consistent with the way of the hood, I resisted (or so I thought). Moving forward, I stopped worrying about public opinion and started doing what felt natural. Even still, I struggled to find myself. For seventeen years my identity had been in the hood. Now it was beginning to feel foreign to me.

Tay and I continued to date throughout my next three years in college. Though we were both African Americans, we came from totally different backgrounds. While I had grown up in the projects and attended predominately black public schools, she was from the suburbs of St. Louis and attended high school at a predominantly white private institution. We exposed each other to new ideas, which helped us learn and grow; but by this time, I had developed too many bad habits. The hood raised me to disrespect women, so I was rude and unapologetic. Though I cared for her, I was too tainted to handle the kind of relationship we were in. Ultimately, my loyalty to "the game" would supersede my loyalty to our relationship, which would lead to its demise.

I turned all my attention to football and did just enough in school to make sure I stayed eligible to play. My senior season concluded and I started preparing for my NFL campaign. The weeks passed quickly and the NFL Draft was finally here. Based on my projections, I knew that if I was drafted, it was not going to be on the first day, but I sat in my apartment and watched as my dream came true for so many other young men. The second day of the draft, I went back home to the projects. Mama cooked and invited a couple family members and close friends over to join us for the special occasion. This was it. All the time and effort I had put in over the years was for this very moment. I was not invited to the NFL Combine (an invite-only camp where top-rated collegiate football players perform physical and mental tests in front of NFL scouts, coaches and general managers), but I had a solid performance at Northwestern's NFL Pro Day (similar to the combine except NFL scouts travel around the country to individual universities), so I was optimistic about my chances of being drafted. As the 4th round of the draft began, I reclined back in the sofa and relaxed as we waited…and waited…and waited. As hours passed, I could feel the tension start to build in the back of my neck, so I stood up to stretch my legs and double checked to make sure the phone was on the hook properly. Finally, an NFL executive approached the podium and said the dreaded seven words, "With the last pick of the draft…" It was all over. I was devastated, but I tried to do everything I could to save face and not show any emotions. I waited until everybody was gone, then I went upstairs to my old bedroom. There in the dark isolated confines of my childhood space, I finally broke down.

Back to Reality

After college, for the first time ever, I felt myself experiencing some slight depression. I had grown very fond of my new lifestyle, but seven rounds of the NFL draft passed without my name being called and the commencement ceremony had concluded. College was over. I had no money in my pockets, just a piece of paper that gave me the potential to earn money in the future, so it was time to head back home to the projects.

As frustration set in, I found myself asking "Why did I even go to college in the first place?" Everything was coming around full circle and I was on my way back to where I started. Even with my degree in my hand, I felt like I had accomplished nothing. Though I had come to Northwestern specifically for the degree, I never intended to put it to use (or at least not for a while). My plan was always to play in the NFL, make enough money to retire, and invest wisely.

Although I didn't get drafted, I was brought into rookie camp with the Dallas Cowboys, but as quickly as rookie camp began; it ended without a contract offer on the table. Ultimately, that would be the extent of my NFL career.

There were many variables that could have contributed to my depressed state. From a nasty breakup, to moving back home, to not making it in the NFL; but I believe depression surfaced because for the first time in my life I had no direction. It was like someone had pulled a rug out from under me. From age ten, football had been a part of my life and the older I became the more my life started to revolve around it. Once I saw that I could potentially earn a scholarship to play in college, all other extracurricular activities were tossed aside. As a young child, I wanted to be an actor, but before that flame could ignite it was extinguished along with everything else. All my time and focus was devoted to training and becoming a student of the game of football. For more than a decade, I would eat, sleep and breathe football. The problem wasn't that I couldn't do anything else; it was that I didn't know anything else.

Unsure of where to turn, and feeling like the world had turned its back on me, I turned to the one person I knew could provide some wisdom and guidance...my grandmother. Granny, as usual, encouraged me to pray. Granny wasn't a very religious person (i.e., she didn't belong to a church), but she believed in God with all her heart. Granny believed all that was needed to follow Christ was a bible and a pair of knees (to pray). She viewed churchgoers as a bunch of hypocrites playing dress-up.

While prayer wasn't the advice I was looking for, I was completely out of ideas, so I decided to give it a try. I started praying daily. I even borrowed Granny's bible periodically. As I began to pray and read the Word, I started to witness a positive change in me. Over the years, I had allowed myself to become someone I didn't recognize. I was arrogant. I was callous. I was selfish and egotistical. But I was determined to get back to being the humble, unselfish and sympathetic child of my youth—before the streets corrupted me. This transformation happened so gradually that I didn't even notice the change. It took something as traumatic as losing my dream to stop me in my tracks and allow me a moment of clarity. As I continued to develop my relationship with God, I started to see clearer and clearer. Insignificant things that I used to deem so important were rendered useless. This spiritual awakening gave me the freedom to live with no regards to how the world viewed me.

Even after attending Northwestern, being exposed to the broader world and experiencing a shift in my perspective, my identity was still in the hood (Robbins). It was my home. As such, I struggled with fully letting go of my street mentality until I developed a relationship with Christ. I found my identity in Him. Then, I know longer felt the need to hold on to the past.

As I continued to pursue God, I also continued to pursue my dream of one day playing in the NFL. I trained in the mornings. In the evenings, I worked part-time as a Youth Development Specialist at Teen Living Programs—a transitional living program for homeless teenagers. Our clients ranged from ages 18 to 21. Most of the male clients were young black men. I saw a lot of myself, as a teen, in them. We were alike in that we all grew up in the hood, but the major difference (which landed me there as an employee and them as a resident) was our family upbringing.

Though I grew up in the hood, I had a loving family that cared for me and always kept my best interest at heart. Between my mother and grandmother, there was always someone there I could count on in time of need. Life wasn't perfect. Sometimes the family even seemed dysfunctional, but through it all, it was never lost upon me how much I was genuinely loved.

I struggled to identify with some of the challenges these young men faced. There were stories of lies and betrayal from parents, physical and sexual abuse by family members. Hurt caused by people who were supposed to be their loved ones. It's a terrible feeling to have to be on guard with your own family. It was tough enough watching over my shoulders in the streets, making sure nobody caught me slippin'. I couldn't imagine having to go home and keep my head on a swivel there too. Home is supposed to be a safe haven—a place where you can feel free to relax and be yourself—not a prison courtyard.

When I first started at TLP, I was only 22 years old, but since I was on staff and I carried myself in a mature manner, all the youth thought I was older. Truthfully, there were at least two young men in the program that were born in the same year as me. Though only months separated us, there was a distinct difference in our maturity level and state of mind.

I was convinced that some of the young men I was working with at the shelter were suffering from a lack of exposure. We were all from the hood, but over the past four years I had traveled all over the United States playing football and studied at one of the premiere universities in the country. I figured if I could somehow impart some of the knowledge I gained over the past few years, it could help further shape their perspective—creating a new outlook and approach to life.

That ideology was the foundation on which this book was formed. Working at TLP taught me 1) there are some very unfit parents in the world 2) living in the hood gives people a false sense of reality 3) there is always someone out there with a story worse than yours and 4) not everybody that is in need of help wants help. I tried to keep these truisms in mind as I worked to complete the manuscript.

After two years of training and periodic tryouts, leading from one dead end to the next, I decided it was time to move forward. I never put a time limit on my NFL pursuit, in fear that I might quit prematurely. Instead, I promised myself that I would pursue it until God showed me otherwise. One day I woke up and felt a strong urge pulling me in another direction. My desire to play the game of football was subsiding, so I decided it was time to start the next chapter in my life.

I wasn't sure where God would take me, but I was looking forward to the journey. Over the years, I had run into many other NFL hopefuls and everybody had a reason why they didn't make it to the NFL; not once did I meet a guy who didn't make it because he wasn't good enough (including me).

Whereas, a lot of athletes transitioned into coaching, personal training or something sports related, I wanted to get as far away as possible. I could not bear to be around football. It was like dating a girl for many years with the expectation of someday getting married and then all of a sudden she dumps you and asks if you would like to still be friends. "No!" You don't want to be friends. You want nothing to do with her.

Maybe some guys would be onboard with just being friends, but, if he really loved her, the first time he saw her with another man that friendship would be over. I had several college teammates who made it to the NFL. I wanted to be happy for them, but I could only be so enthusiastic watching them play with me on the outside looking in. Watching the NFL was no longer exciting to me; it was a constant reminder of my failure.

I was offered a position as a Management Trainee for a railroad transportation company in Norfolk Virginia. I didn't know the first thing about the rail industry. I wasn't even convinced that cargo still shipped via rail, but it was a great opportunity for me to start my post-football career.

At the time, I was still in the dating stage with my wife, Leanne. I was a little concerned about our relationship. I worried that if I left without any real commitment our relationship would not survive the long distance. Then, I asked myself if I could live with that outcome. The answer was a resounding "No!" We had only been dating for about a year and a half, but over that short period of time our relationship had quickly blossomed into something very serious. At this point I was deeply in love with her and addicted to the positive impact she had on my life. She made me strive to be a better person, man, son and friend. She touched my life in a way that no other girlfriend had—quickly becoming one of the most significant persons in my life. She was caring and nurturing. She was smart and open-minded. She was a woman of faith—strong and unwavering. All the qualities I wanted and needed in a woman she possessed in abundance.

I took all the money I had saved and went to the jewelry store. I bought a small one-third carat diamond ring and took the rest of the money and put it down on a three-day cruise to the Bahamas. Then I called my wife's father and asked for his daughter's hand in marriage. He said, "Yes" so I proceeded with my plans. I called her job and secretly requested three days off. The day before the cruise I had flowers delivered to her job. The note attached read, "Pack your bags, we're headed to the Bahamas!" She called me hysterical trying to figure out what was going on. I downplayed it as a surprise going-away trip before I left for my new job.

The stage was set, but while I was running around picking up some last minute items for the trip, I received an alarming phone call from my mother saying that my grandmother had to be rushed to the hospital. Granny had suffered some form of a heart attack. After several failed attempts to stabilize her, the doctors had given up. I made it to the hospital just in time for a doctor to walk into the waiting room and pronounce my grandmother dead. I was speechless. Here I was planning an engagement trip to the Bahamas as Granny was taking her last breath. As I sat in the emergency room waiting on my mother to finish signing all the necessary paperwork, I couldn't help but to reflect on the impact my grandmother's presence had on my life. Throughout all the variable circumstances in my life, she had been that one constant—vote of confidence, caregiver, attitude adjuster, unconditional lover.

I would have postponed the engagement trip, but with me leaving for Virginia in a couple weeks this was my only chance. I proposed to Leanne the first night onboard the ship; we used the rest of the trip to celebrate our engagement. We enjoyed the entire experience, but when we docked, I came home and buried my grandmother. After the funeral, I packed my bags and left for Virginia.

From attending Northwestern, I was used to being one of the few minorities, but joining the railroad industry added another dimension. I was not only a racial minority, but I was also one of the younger employees in the company—I was an age minority. A great deal of my colleagues had been with the company more years than I had been on this earth. It was a "good ol' boy" industry heavily dominated by white males. Many of whom were second and third generation "railroaders."

In a span of six years, I went from living in an all-black community, to attending a predominantly white university, to working in a white-male dominated industry. While my life had done a complete 180, in the process, I learned who I am and throughout it all I've maintained a strong sense of self.

My plan was to work in the corporate world for about five years then branch out on my own. In the interim time I would gain some experience and put aside as much money as possible to start my own business. Ultimately, I knew I wanted to be a professional writer because I'm addicted to writing (in any capacity). I enjoy writing and rewriting sentences until I properly convey the message I intend. I'm never satisfied with using some generic word to describe an emotion or scene. I want to use the word that best describes my feelings (even if that means scouring the dictionary and using an eight letter word). All this led me to the conclusion that I needed to start my own publishing company.

I found my creative niche. None of which would have happened had I continued playing football. In hind sight, I look back on the path I took to arrive at this point and I can only laugh because I fought so hard to keep my football dreams alive out of fear of failure. Had I known what would rise out of the depths of my failure, I would have accepted my fate much sooner. Writing has given me the same pleasure as football. But I appreciate it more now that I know what it feels like to have something you love stripped away from you. I take comfort in the fact that me and writing can grow old together.

3

DEFYING THE LAW OF POVERTY

Law of Poverty: if you were born poor, you will remain poor
and ultimately die poor

Generically speaking, the law of gravity states, "what goes up must come down and it will freefall at a rate of 9.8 m/s²," therefore, it was once believed that man would never be able to create a flying object. In 2011 Air Traffic Control reported more than 50 million take-offs and landings for the year. That is the law of gravity being defied 50 million times.

The law of poverty states, "if you were born poor, you will remain poor and ultimately die poor." This unspoken law has proven to be true for many years. Throughout hoods across the country, second and third generations of families remain impoverished. For every person who has risen above poverty, there are hundreds more that remain impoverished. That is equivalent to saying for every successful take-off there are hundreds of airplanes that crash daily. If that were the case, airplanes would not be a commercial means of transportation. Until a method is discovered to consistently and effectively defy the law of poverty, regardless of periodical breakthroughs, the problem will never be resolved.

It can take generations to remove the curse of poverty from an entire family, but the process starts with the sacrifice of one courageous individual. It requires someone to make a stand and say, "It stops right here!"

Before you can defy the law of poverty, you must first understand what poverty is and how it works. It seems elementary, on the surface, but if you take a deeper dive into the issues you will quickly realize the complexities of poverty.

What is poverty? By definition poverty is: the state or condition of having little or no money, goods, or means of support. However, the definition varies depending on who is being asked the question. Some define it quantitatively, measuring the total household income against the poverty-line; while others define it qualitatively, basing it purely on a person's quality of life. I tend to side more with the qualitative approach. The quantitative definition is not specific enough. It doesn't take into consideration the varying degrees of poverty. There are some households that are flirting with the poverty line and then there are those in deep poverty. I define poverty as: living in the lowest social class with a lack of necessities (food, clothes, shelter, etc.) for which you either go without or require government assistance to meet your needs.

In reality, that is the definition of US poverty. Third-world poverty means there is no government assistance. People go days without food to eat, or fresh water to drink. In America, we generally associate poverty with living in the hood or growing up in the projects. While it may not be as challenging as poverty in some other countries, overcoming US poverty is challenging in its own way.

In the hood, it's all about survival. When you look outside, in every direction, all you see is poverty; hustle man on the corner selling bootleg CDs, dope boys on the block yelling, "2 for 15." People are doing whatever it takes to survive another day...another week... another year. Living in the hood is much like being in prison. You might not be physically behind bars, but you are financially handcuffed, which creates an imaginary barrier that stretches around the entire community.

Often when prisoners are released from the penitentiary after serving a long sentence, they have a hard time adjusting back to the outside world. Similarly, soldiers who return home after years at war, have a difficult time assimilating back into civilian life. The reason is that both the prisoner and the soldier were a part of a subculture, or a group of people with a culture that differs from the culture at large. When they return home the dynamics change and it is difficult for them to adapt to the new customs.

Poverty is a subculture. People who live in poverty usually live in concentrated areas of the city, away from the mass population. Within those imaginary four walls, the rules and regulations deviate significantly from that of the larger culture. Like the military and prison, living in poverty requires you to develop a distinct mindset in order to survive. That mindset encourages inhabitants to settle for less, accept their fate and live below their potential.

Public housing and government welfare programs only encourage this mentality. Public housing was created to provide transitional living for the lower-class, yet many take something that was supposed to be temporary and turn it into their permanent dwelling. Government welfare is only meant to bridge the gap, yet some attempt to use it to provide a living. Why? Because there is a system in place that provides just enough comfort to keep lesser ambitious people from striving for more.

I would like to see poverty one day become extinct, but the reality is that day will never come. We live in a "survival of the fittest" capitalist society where most trade, industry and means of production are owned by individuals or corporations (unlike in a communist system, in which the government controls the major means of production). If you are familiar with economics and the concept of capitalism, you understand that within the system, the rich and poor are mutually important. Both are needed in order for the system to work. If everyone was wealthy, no blue collar jobs would exist. Who would be left to drive trucks so products can get to market? Pick up garbage? Clean public bathrooms, or serve you at your favorite fast-food restaurant? The structure of our economy is based on the ideology that poor or lower-class citizens will always exist, but that doesn't mean you have to remain a part of that socioeconomic class.

Our economic system, in addition to welfare aiding in the perpetuation of poverty, is an indictment on our government against poor people. When you have a specific race of people (African Americans) that are disproportionately poorer than another, it appears like an indictment on our government against black people. I'm not a conspiracy theorist who believes that our government is deliberately trying to keep African Americans living as second-class citizens, but that is ultimately the result. Now that you understand that there are forces, intentionally or unintentionally, working to keep you impoverished, find a way to buck the trend. Join the rest of the elite alumni from the school of hard knocks who defied the law of poverty and changed their narrative.

Build a Spiritual Foundation

I know this may be a touchy subject for some readers; however, I could not talk about how to defy the law of poverty and how to live a more meaningful life without covering this topic.

We live in a fragile world, where plans that seem foolproof are not; time that appears guaranteed is not. We walk around as though we were granted an 80 or 90 year life span, but in reality death is unpredictable. You could walk out of your house today and never return. I say this not to scare you, but to encourage you to use what precious time you have here on earth wisely. Building a strong spiritual foundation will help you keep life in proper perspective.

As a teenager, whenever I thought about surrendering my life to Christ, I would say to myself "I'm too young! I gotta have my fun first, then I'll give my life to God when I'm older." On the surface, it appears that by choosing to walk with God you will miss out on the "fun in life"; but contrary to popular belief, life gets even better. I compare choosing to walk with God to choosing to eat healthy.

As a youngster, it wasn't odd for me to eat two Hostess iced honey buns for breakfast or lunch, but as a collegiate athlete I had to improve my diet to get my body into peak form. Like most people, I was under the misconception that if I change my diet and start eating healthy I wouldn't enjoy food anymore. I would be forced to eat rice cakes and drink beet juice and miss out on the "finer foods in life," but that's far from the truth. It's not so much what you eat at all; it's how the food is prepared. Once you get beyond all your preconceived notions about healthy eating, you begin to realize that there is no excuse to still be cooking with lard, or eating fried food for every meal. There are healthier alternatives like using olive or canola oil instead of lard and grilling or baking instead of frying. The real eye opener is when you start to substitute healthier cooking habits and realize that you actually enjoy the taste better. Similarly, when you begin walking with God, you will realize that you actually enjoy life better.

This walk is not one without roadblocks. I face adversity every day. Most times the adversary is myself. By nature, we are all sinners, but by birth we are also the children of God. Christ died on the cross for our sins. Therefore, all sins are forgiven for those who accept Christ as Lord and Savior. Ephesians 1:7 reads "In Him we have redemption through His blood, the forgiveness of sins, in accordance with the riches of God's grace..." A good friend of mine put it best. He said, "As Christians, we tend to think of forgiveness in the present tense. You do something wrong and say, 'Forgive me Lord!' or you say something wrong and say, 'Forgive me Lord!' but God's forgiveness is eternal." He is the Alpha and the Omega (beginning and the end). Thus, you've already been forgiven for your future sins—five, ten, even fifteen years from now. If you've witnessed Christians walking around looking condemned (or condemning others), it's because they haven't truly grasped this concept. This revelation will set you free. You will stop hanging your head every time you fall short. You will stop viewing premarital sex, drinking alcohol or using profanity as the forbidden fruit—making it more desirable. You will stop living life trying not to mess up and live life with the understanding that no sin is too great to be forgiven by God. You will chose to obey God's word out of love for Him, not out of fear of damnation.

A walk with God is not perfect, but it is one that you have to be committed to wholeheartedly. Regardless of your shortcomings or how many times you fall, you have to be willing to get back up again and press forward.

This walk is not one you can follow without faith. By faith I mean putting your trust in God and believing that He will provide for you when logic suggests otherwise. Sometimes you have to throw logic out the window. This book is chalked full of logical thoughts and suggestions that should help you on your path to success. I did my best to cover as much information as possible, but the truth is I don't have a clue what God has in store for your life. The tricky thing about life is that the logical choice is not always the correct one. This is where wisdom from above is necessary to help guide your steps.

You might be living in the hood in an unimaginable situation. Your home might double as a crack house. Both your parents might be drug addicts. All logic suggests that you are in a no-win situation. You are bound to poverty for the rest of your life. The best you can hope for is to not become addicted to drugs yourself. But you are a gifted student with dreams of becoming a heart surgeon. Your relationship with a mentor helped you avoid some of the strongholds and pitfalls that could have killed your dream. You received a scholarship to attend Stanford University. You go on to finish med school, residency and start a private practice—becoming one of the top surgeons in your field. Logically, this makes no sense; the odds were against you avoiding drugs let alone rising above poverty.

With God anything is possible, but you have to trust Him and keep the faith. Just because one door shuts in your face that doesn't mean God won't open another one. The problem sometimes is that people get so fixated on one goal that they fail to realize other opportunities that are being presented. I'm not advocating that you prematurely give up on your dreams because you face adversity; I'm suggesting that you develop a relationship with God, because only He can advise you whether you should be going over the mountain or around it.

Become Whole

I would be remiss, if I did not acknowledge the fact that there are some young people out there hurting from a childhood of neglect. Whether it was abandonment, or some form of abuse, these are all very heinous acts. Harboring this pain inside, for any length of time, can take its toll on your body. Until you are able to rid yourself of past hurts, you will never be able to fully move forward with your life.

Often, we only pay attention to what is seen, but what is even more harmful is the unseen. If you fell and scraped your knee on the concrete and it started to bleed, you would probably clean it and cover it with a Band-Aid. Truthfully, had you not done anything to treat the scrape, it would have healed and you would have been just fine (barring some life threatening infection). Now let's say you were in a minor car accident and unknowingly suffered blunt force trauma to the abdominal area, causing severe damage to an internal organ. If you made the mistake of going home rather than to an emergency room, because there was no visible sign of injury, you could potentially die in a the matter of hours due to internal bleeding.

Some of you are living with internal bleeding and the longer it takes you to receive proper treatment, the more damage it will cause to your health. Before you can defy the law of poverty, you have to make sure you are whole.

If no one else on this earth displays love and genuine care for your well being, at least the woman that birthed you is supposed to… right? There is no greater pain than the feeling of being unwanted by your mother. Dealing with resentment caused by the rejection of a parent requires healing. Built up anger will not disappear, it will only be displaced. Anger and bitterness towards a parent or family member will manifest itself in other areas. Stop holding all the anger and resentment inside. Get help!

Overcoming abandonment and abuse is a process. There are necessary steps you must take in order to successfully move forward with your life. Unfortunately, this book will not touch on this topic, but building a solid spiritual foundation will help you cleanse your heart and walk in a spirit of happiness. There are also other books that address these issues and professionals who can help you deal specifically with your issues and bring closure to a dysfunctional childhood.

Think Outside da Block

Living in the hood, you are taught how the world operates through the lens of an impoverished environment. But the way people operate within the hood does not necessarily coincide with the mass society. In order to rise above poverty, you will have to recondition your mind. Your outlook on life has been drastically shaped by your surroundings. Everything from how to dress, how to get money, to how to date, has been influenced by the hood.

Back in high school my best friend Travis and I went out with these two girls and ditched them at the movies. We drove to their house to pick them up. When we got there they insisted we ride with them, so we jumped in their car and headed to the movies. Once we got to the theater, Travis and I already knew the drill, we were going to purchase two tickets and have one person come back out and hand the ticket stubs off to the other two people. Usually the ticket attendant never asked the person who just left the theater to show their stub to re-enter. But when we proposed the plan to the ladies they were appalled. We argued back and forth for a second then we gave them two options, either sneak in with us, or buy your own tickets. They chose the latter.

After paying for their tickets they headed right towards the concession stand and requested that we buy them popcorn and drinks. Travis and I looked at each other and respectfully declined their demand. We weren't hungry so we headed into the theater while they waited in line for some refreshments. They finally made it into the theater as the opening credits were concluding. At this point we knew the night was ruined, so we made a bold attempt to salvage the night for ourselves. We were at the point of no return with these girls, so Travis went outside and called one of our other homeboys to come scoop us. Travis came back in the theater and told the girls his mother had a flat tire and she needed help. They knew we were full of crap because we didn't even have our car with us, but right in the middle of the movie we walked out and left them. Our homeboy came and picked us up and took us back to our car. The night was still young, so we called two girls that we had met earlier that day at the mall and hung out with them instead.

At the time we laughed and made jokes about the situation. Looking back on it now that I'm older and more mature, this was the epitome of chauvinism and disrespect. But this was how the streets raised us to treat women. "The game" taught us if you trick money on a chick, you're a lame. If you show too much kindness, you're a "sucka for love." If you let them, women will use you. It was either play or get played, so we elected to be on the positive side of the equation.

There was a guy I grew up with who was a part of my outer-circle of friends. Like me, he was raised by a single-mother and was taught to treat women with respect. The difference is that his mother did a better job of sheltering him from all the outside influences that lead me astray. In high school, he was known for having a lot of female friends, of which he was not sexually active with—nor did he appear to be actively pursuing. "The game" taught us to seek and destroy, but he was genuinely interested in them as friends. He was often ridiculed and made to feel like less of a man for not having an ulterior motive for befriending these young ladies. Due to his relationship with them, and the genuine interest he showed in their well-being, he was nicknamed "The Pink Bunny"–our best attempt to emasculate him.

It took me a long time to figure out what it means to be a man (and

I'm still learning). One thing I realized is that in order to find my queen I had to recondition my mind. I disregarded all the misconceptions I was taught about women growing up in the hood. I stopped allowing the hood to dictate my thoughts and developed my own opinion. My old approach to dating was helpful while I was playing the field and not looking for anything serious, but to find my soul mate I had to learn to trust and be trustworthy.

Some of you young ladies that are being groomed by older sisters, cousins or even your mother on how "the game" works will need to part ways with those misguided thoughts. Using your body like it's a good to be traded for money or a service is a zero-sum game. If you play your cards wrong, you end up a poor single mother on welfare with four kids—all by different men. If you play your cards right, this approach might land you the biggest baller in the neighborhood, but what it will never do is bring you long-term happiness. You forfeit all your rights as a human being when you auction off your body to the highest bidder.

Whether it's in reference to relationships, how you walk, how you talk, or how you view the world, there is a process you must go through to successfully recondition your mind. First, you have to recognize and acknowledge the fact that your thoughts and beliefs have been somewhat distorted by your upbringing—the narrow view of the world you've observed from the hood is merely a glimpse. Secondly, you have to be open to the idea of a new way of thinking. That doesn't mean you have to completely abandon your beliefs, but you have to be open-minded. Thirdly, you have to expose yourself to the world outside of the hood. More exposure to the outside world will further shape your perspective on life—this is the best way to force yourself to think outside da block.

For instance, when my wife and I first met, she thought it was strange that I had my mother's last name. Most of my friends growing up had their mother's last name, so this didn't strike me as odd. The more we talked about it; we started to realize it was a social class issue. My wife grew up in a middle-class suburb in Southern California, where most of her friends' parents were married at some point; thus the children were given the last name of their father. In my neighborhood it was not uncommon for brothers and sisters to live down the street from one another. With fathers working their way down the block like garbage men and no wedding bells to speak of. It only made sense to give children the last name of their mother; otherwise, you could potentially have a household of three or four siblings all with different last names. This revelation was only revealed to me by having a conversation with someone from a different socioeconomic status— my wife saw the world from a different vantage point.

Last but not least, after you've gained more exposure, re-examine your views on life—attempt to separate the product (you) from the environment. Take inventory of your thoughts. Look in the mirror and ask yourself, "Who am I? What's important to me? Why is it important?" Try to drill down to your inner-being in its simplest form. Those thoughts that remain in agreement with your core beliefs hold on to them. If you find there are some beliefs that are at odds with your new outlook, get rid of those thoughts!

Create a Value System

We've all heard the expression, "You can't do it all," so developing a value system is important in working towards your goals. If you are an heiress to a multi-billion dollar hotel chain then you might have the luxury to waste time partying and drinking all day and night, but if you are the heiress to a multi-job working mother who has little to no savings in the bank, you need to act accordingly. Any wealth that is created will arrive by your own doing.

Life is all about choices and sacrifice. You can't do it all, so you have to make choices, and with these choices less important time-consumers have to be sacrificed. That's why it is absolutely imperative to keep your priorities in order and understand what is most important to you.

We have to live like we're dying. Ask yourself, "If I knew I only had a year left to live, would I be spending my time doing this?" Too often it takes a tragedy or some life altering event to change our behavior or actions. If you're living your life to the fullest and keeping your priorities in order, even in the face of death your actions will remain relatively unchanged. That's how you know you're priorities are in proper prospective.

Don't be a puppet. Have a mind of your own. Don't allow your environment to dictate your beliefs. The hood will have you believing that sex, money and drugs are the keys to life—even if you believe otherwise. Your mind can be socialized into believing that these things are desirable and important. This will cause you to waste valuable time chasing after worldly desires, not the desires of your heart.

If you were to interview a group of convicted felons, and ask, "If you could do it all over again, would you still commit the crime?" the majority would say "No." Maybe it's because they're remorseful, but it's more likely because of their current circumstance. Ten years from now you probably won't regret all the partying, drinking and time wasted, but you will look at your current circumstance and wish you had another chance. In life there are no "do-overs," only "do-going-forwards." You can't change the past, but you can decide your future.

Depending on how strict or flexible your parents are, your value system and moral standards might need to be higher than the ones set forth by your parents. If you don't have a curfew, set one. If your mother thinks seventeen is old enough to start having sex, respectfully disagree. Parents can be physically mature, yet immature in mind. It's not that they mean you any harm. It's just that they have become jaded by their own surroundings and experiences. Sometimes parents take on the "What's good for me is good for them" philosophy. If Dad used to drink liquor as a teenager or run with a gang, he believes it's "harmless" to his children. That's when finding a mentor, someone outside of your parents who can give you proper guidance, becomes crucial.

Eliminate Distractions

If you have friends who are not serious about life, ones who only want to crack jokes and laugh all day, I suggest you part ways with them. They will only distract you from your goals. At the end of the day, when all the laughing and joking stops you will still be poor and struggling. Studies show that you will earn the same salary as your four closest friends, so if I were you I would choose to hang around people who are moving in a positive direction.

I'm often asked, "How did you find time to write while working full-time?" It's simple. I cut back on watching TV. For you it might be cutting back on talking on the phone, texting, or listening to music. You would be amazed at how many hours there are in a day if you woke up early and limited TV, video games, social networks and other unproductive activities.

Leisure time is good as long as it is not excessive. We all need a break from the real world from time-to-time, to allow our minds to relax and indulge in mindless activity. The brain is a muscle, so after intense exercise, it requires recovery time just like any other muscle. However, if your leisure activity is preventing you from effectively pursuing your dreams, it is a distraction.

Television presents the biggest challenge for me because there are a variety of different shows, movies and sports I can watch. No matter how I'm feeling, I can find something on TV to complement my mood. If I'm in a competitive mood, a good football game is the answer. If I'm bored and need a little excitement, a good action movie will do the trick; or if I'm struggling to fall asleep, one of my wife's chick flicks will work miracles.

If you're like me, watching TV works for any occasion, but have you ever put watching TV into perspective? If you have, you probably are no longer struggling with your TV obsession. One day I was sitting around in deep thought. I had the TV on a football game, as usual, but only as background noise. I was thinking about my future and the next steps to starting-up a business, when all of a sudden it hit me "Why are you wasting so much time watching TV?" Think about it...from the moment you power on your television, every person that you see is doing a job, whether they are an actor, actress, reality show host, news anchor, politician, music artist, coach or athlete. Every person is being paid for their services. These people are living out their dreams and "what are you doing?" watching them from the sideline. It's time to get off the bench and get in the game!

Adapt To Your Environment

In Robbins, during the summer of 2004 (over a 2 month period), seven young men were shot (3 fatal) less than 100 meters away from each other. To put it in perspective, in the same distance it would take the fastest man in the world roughly 9.6 seconds to cover, 3 people lost their lives and 4 were wounded. The only other time men die at such a rate in such close proximity is in war, thus I would consider my neighborhood to have been a "war zone"!

My older brother had the misfortune or fortune, depending on how you look at it, of being one of the young men wounded. He's fortunate that he was not one of the fatalities, but unfortunately he has to live with the mental and emotional trauma for the rest of his life (not to mention the bullet lodged in his back adjacent to his spinal cord.)

My mother had the joy of being awakened, on her birthday, at 4am and informed by a perfect stranger that her son had been shot. It was certainly not the way she had anticipated celebrating her 46th birthday, but there she was in her bath robe walking across the street to her son—my brother—sitting on the sidewalk with a bullet in his leg and back. It was not until she looked in the distance to a young man lying dead in the street that she realized she had received the birthday gift of a lifetime.

As sensational and dramatic as this story sounds, the storyline is truly unremarkable. Periodically throughout the summer in Chicago, the local news will lead off with this top story of the night, "4 dead, 15 wounded" or "9 dead, 30 wounded." It's usually a drive-by shooting with some gang or drug affiliation. Often amongst the dead and injured are innocent bystanders—undeserving of their fate.

Let's say you enlisted in the service and were shipped off to war. Then, you were dropped in the center of hostile warfare. Everyone in your unit was killed and you were the sole survivor. Would you purposely draw attention to yourself? No, you would lay low and do whatever it took to stay alive until the choppers came to rescue you.

By the same token, if your neighborhood is a war zone and you know wearing the color red or blue will draw the wrong attention, wear white. If you know that wearing your hat to the right or the left will draw attention, don't wear one at all. Notice I didn't say where your hat straight. I said, "DON'T WEAR ONE AT ALL." How often do you turn on the local news and hear about somebody getting killed due to mistaken identity?

In a war zone there is a very thin line between life and death. You can be a daredevil and choose to flirt with that line, or you can attempt to avoid it all together. No one can provide you with a foolproof way to stay alive. Even sitting on your front porch can be fatal. Sometimes innocent people get caught in the crossfire. All you can do is try to put yourself in the best possible position to survive. I guarantee if you dressed like a country music singer with a cowboy hat, jeans and a sleeveless flannel no one would mistake you for a gang member. You might not have "swag," but at least you would be safer.

Avoid places where gangs and other troublemakers hangout. Find activities to keep you occupied. Too much free time on your hands equals trouble. Stick to school, any extracurricular activities and home. I coached football for a couple years at a high school in Chicago's inner-city. We had little to no funding for the program, so having enough equipment to outfit the players was a task in and of itself. We would usually collect equipment at the end of practice every day, but we allowed the players who walked home to keep their equipment. They had to walk through some pretty rough neighborhoods and they didn't want to be mistaken as gang members. It's unfortunate that you cannot walk down the street without being harassed by people, but if that is the reality of the situation; you have to adapt to your environment. If I could do it all over again I would trade in my Tims for a pair of cowboy boots…well maybe not cowboy boots, but definitely some Doc Martens.

Develop a Winning Attitude

A wise young man once told me, "I'd rather sit down and look up at life than stand up and look down at it." These were the profound words of Rasul "Rocky" Clark, a young man who suffered a catastrophic spinal cord injury while playing high school football resulting in paralysis and confinement to a wheelchair. His point was valid in that people handicap themselves by their attitude towards life.

Rocky faced adversity everyday just in his will to live. Something as simple as him drinking a glass of water or scratching an itch on his forehead required assistance. Rocky lost all his physical ability. This forced him—a very self-motivated and independent person— to rely on others to do for him what he previously did for himself. Can you imagine the mental and emotional pain? It likely surpassed the frequent physical pain he suffered due to his injury. Rocky was only 16 years old when he was faced with this life-changing event. He lived for another 11 years after his injury before passing in early 2012. Over those 11 years he finished high school, enrolled in college, coached varsity football, mentored young men, wrote poetry and drew pictures (using computer software that allowed him to use his mouth). More importantly, he did it all with a smile. Never once did he want to be looked at as handicapped and because of his attitude and his remarkable courage, no one who knew him ever considered him handicapped.

Rocky was a blessing in my life. I hope his story will bless you as well. He had no control over what happened to him, but he could control how he responded to his circumstance. Rocky chose to be positive and let no hardship stop him from pursuing his life goals. For any of you young people walking around with your head down feeling like your situation couldn't be any worse, imagine how Rocky must have felt.

Like Rocky, you had no control over the impoverished environment you were born into; but as long as you have breath in your lungs and blood circulating through your body, you have the ability to change your situation. It all starts with your attitude. And having a positive attitude is a choice.

Picture yourself driving your brand new BMW 745 up to your 5,000 square foot mansion. Visualize yourself walking past your luxury kitchen, sitting down on your Italian leather sofa and watching TV on your customized 72" screen. Can you see it? Is it clear to you?

Now picture yourself chasing the bus to make sure you're not late for school. Imagine pulling an all-nighter to finish a 20 page paper. Envision sitting alone in your room on the weekend working on your 5-year plan. See into the future. Picture working an entry level job, putting in 12 hour days, working holidays and being significantly underpaid for your services. When you can picture both scenarios and get mutually excited, that's when you know you have a winning attitude. That's when owning a BMW and a 5,000 square foot mansion transform from fantasy to reality.

Find Your Gift(s)

From childhood I've always loved sports, so as I entered high school and started to show potential as a football player, it was a natural progression for me to pursue a career in professional football. Unfortunately, some people do not uncover their talents as effortlessly.

In fact, some of you struggle so hard to identify a specific talent that you assume you don't have any. Everyone on this earth has a special gift. Guys, contrary to popular belief you don't have to dribble your way out the hood—or run a slant-post for that matter. Young ladies, you don't have to sex your way out of the hood. You don't have to find a man with money and depend on him to provide for you what you can provide for yourself. You just need to find your gift. It might be in the arts, sciences, politics, mathematics, etc. You might be a gifted motivational speaker with an uncanny ability to inspire people. You might use this gift to become a coach, minister, or politician. You might be a gifted listener. Friends find you easy to talk to and confide in. This rare quality might direct you into the field of psychiatry, social work, or crisis negotiation. There are endless talents with infinite paths you can take to utilize your gift.

Something as simple as having strong faith can be a gift (talent). Faith is being sure of what you hope for and certain of what you have not seen. Those who display extreme faith approach life as if what they are hoping for has already been rewarded to them; it's just a matter of time before they reap their inheritance.

It's like a child who knows he has millions of dollars in a trust fund that he can start tapping into once he reaches the age of eighteen. He's not going to wait until he has the money to start planning. His plans will have already been set in motion during the years leading up to his eighteenth birthday.

It's important that you protect your gift and don't allow anyone to pervert it. If you are a talented dancer, don't become a stripper. If you were born with breathtaking beauty and your dream is to become a model, don't settle for video vixen or a groupie in some rapper's entourage.

Gifts are to be exercised; you either use them or watch them waste away. Playing into someone else's plans for your life does nothing to cultivate your gift. Don't be a pawn in someone else's chess match. Fight for your dreams. Don't allow anyone or anything to lead you astray.

Dream Big!

Don't ever believe that just because you were raised in poverty you have to limit your goals in life. Your goals should be so lofty that they are almost unimaginable. If your goals are imaginable, they're not big enough. A good way to measure if your goals are high enough is if you tell people about them and they laugh at you. That's a good indicator of larger-than-life goals. People can laugh, but the only way your goals will turn into a joke is if you don't support them with actions; otherwise, there is nothing stopping you from achieving them. You are only limited by your ambitions.

You have the same ability to succeed as any child growing up in white suburbia. It may appear as if you are starting life from a disadvantaged position, but it is only a perception. I like to use the track & field analogy. In track & field, a staggered position only appears that you are at a disadvantage. The track is the same distance around no matter what lane you are running in. The key is to not focus on the person in front of you and just run your own race. Block everyone else out and run as hard as you can. When you cross the finish line and look around...who knows? You might have won the race.

There are other variables in a race that dictate the outcome that has little to do with your lane assignment and everything to do with the talent and ability of the person. Those variables represent the unique qualities in people like IQ, leadership skills, and ambition which separate champions from runner-ups. If you put Usain Bolt (World's Fastest Man) in any lane, it's more than likely he's going to win the race just based on sheer ability.

Your talent, ability and drive will dictate how far you go in life. If you are someone with God-given intelligence and leadership skills, there is no reason why some slacker in white suburbia should beat you in a race to the White House.

Find Support Beams (Mentors)

If you are living in a single parent home, make no mistake about it, there is a void in your life. The people who have made it out of poverty successfully understood that there was a void and found someone in the form of a mentor to help fill that void. It's the people who don't recognize that there is a void who find themselves lost. You have to be receptive to help in order for someone to help you. You cannot defy the laws of poverty on your own, so lose the "me against the world attitude" and accept the help.

Of all the mentors I've had throughout my lifetime, there were many other young men who crossed their paths who they could have affected the same, but these young men saw no value in mentorship. I did, and for that I am a better person. We all need older (wiser) people in our lives to help show us the way. Ideally these people should be your parents, but if your parents are not good examples, find someone else.

When the term "mentor" is used, people often assume that person has to be some prominent figure like a lawyer, pastor, or principal but that person can be anyone you choose him or her to be. I was never a part of any formal mentoring programs. I met my first mentor in the seventh grade. He worked at my middle school. He was not the principal, nor was he a teacher. He wasn't one of the basketball coaches, or even security. He was the janitor.

His name was Michael Watson, but everyone referred to him as "Mike the Janitor." One day my best friend, Travis, and I stayed after school talking to Mike while he cleaned the classrooms. Mike was in his late twenties or early thirties. He was young enough that he still understood our struggles. We could talk to Mike about anything. Any question we asked, he answered. He never censored or tamed down his response because we were kids, he gave it to us uncut and raw. Hours passed as Mike went from class to class cleaning and we were still there. To help him get his tasks done a little faster we decided to pitch in and help. We went into the rest of the classrooms and emptied the trash, wiped down the windows and straightened the desks. Afterwards, all Mike had to do is sweep and mop the floors.

This became our daily routine. Mike split the classrooms in half and gave us trash, windows and desks straightening responsibilities. Travis and I would race to see who could get done the fastest. Afterwards, we would go play basketball in the gymnasium. Over the years, we must have played more than a thousand one-on-one games. We would go at it for hours, pushing and shoving until it was time for Mike to clean the gym. Then we would go into the library and pop in a movie. Usually at some point Mike's girlfriend would show up with food and we would eat, finish watching the movie and head home. Most mornings I would leave for school at 7:30am and would not get back home until around 9:00pm.

There was nothing spectacular or special about what Mike did. It didn't require a whole lot of extra effort on his part. He showed us love and gave us something to do. When you're young, half of the foolish mistakes you make are due to the fact that you're bored.

The school was a safe haven. It provided a healthy alternative to the streets. If we did something foolish at school, it wouldn't cost us our lives. Our after-school program with Mike lasted from the seventh grade until the end of our freshman year in high school.

Shortly after graduating from the eighth grade, I met a young and very ambitious high school football coach. He had received word from some of his players from the neighborhood, that I was one of the up and coming talents. He began his recruiting efforts through my sister. She would often bring messages home from school. One day while he was in the projects picking up some of the other players, we met. He introduced himself as Coach Williams. He was only twenty-four years old and the lone black football coach on staff. We connected instantaneously. Because of his age, he felt more like a big brother than a father figure. He was young enough that he still embraced the culture of my generation—slang, fashion, music.

Over my first year of high school, Coach Williams and I became very close. He stepped into the role of mentor. This was not like the changing of the guard, or something that happens overnight. It took a year or so for a full transition to occur. In the interim, I relied on both Mike and Coach Williams for guidance and sound advice, but Coach Williams was the person I conversed with daily. By the end of my freshman year, all mentoring responsibilities had been shifted from Mike the Janitor to Coach Williams.

Even though Coach Williams was my coach, our relationship stretched far beyond the football field. We would talk during the school day, hang out on the weekend and if I ever needed him, he was only a phone call away. We could talk about anything from sports to music, but the thing I valued most about our relationship was his faith in me. I've always believed in myself, but to have someone stand in agreement with me, provided much needed reassurance. As a skinny 5'10" 165 pound freshman, he told me, "You have a rare talent. Before you graduate, every school in the country will be recruiting you." Like clockwork, by my junior year the letters started to pour in.

My senior year, Coach Williams left the school. He took a coaching position at another high school and as before, the mentoring responsibilities started to shift.

This time it was the neighborhood barber, but anyone who has ever sat in Otis' chair knows he was much more than a barber. He was an R&B singer, sports analyst, preacher, broker, and politician. Depending on the day, when you sat down in his chair, he would provide you with some words of wisdom, sell you some used tires, or bet against you on a football game. If it was a really good day, he might even serenade you with a song—whether you liked it or not.

The barber shop was called Unique—a fitting name due to the different personalities that occupied this shop over the years. I had been getting my haircut at Unique since I was a little kid. I first met Otis when he came in as a new barber to the neighborhood shop. He was a young man in his early twenties. I was a freshman in high school. Like most new barbers, he spent more time sitting in his own chair than anyone else. One day I walked in and before I could take a seat, he pointed at me.

"You need a haircut?" I paused, because I didn't want him to cut my hair, but I wasn't sure how to tell him.

"Yeah." I said.

"Come on," he replied, so I walked apprehensively towards his chair and took a seat.

I don't remember being overly impressed with my haircut, but I do remember leaving the shop thinking, "Man, that cat was deep." I was only in the chair about fifteen minutes, but it felt like three hours. In that time, we learned each other's background and talked about the future. I explained to him that I was going to be the next Walter Payton, as he told me his plans of running his own barbershop.

"How are your grades?"

"I'm a B student," I stated with confidence.

The next time I came in for a haircut, after he finished, I tried handing him the money my mother gave me for the haircut, but he wouldn't take it.

"As long as you keep your grades up, your money is no longer good here," he said.

I thought he was joking, so I would still try and pay him, but time after time he would not accept the money. This went on for over four years until I left for college. Some days, Otis would open the shop at the crack of dawn, just so Travis and I could get haircuts before school, knowing that we had no money to compensate him. In fact, sometimes he would give us money. Unless you were the bootleg man and sold DVDs, or you "made a come up" shooting craps in the back room of the barbershop, it was highly unlikely that you would leave the shop with more money than you came with, but I often did. I would come in for a haircut for the Homecoming dance and leave with money to take my date out to eat.

More than the free haircuts and the money, I valued Otis' relationship because he shared my enthusiasm for life. We both had the courage to dream big. I would bounce ideas off of him and he would listen and encourage. Then he would match my idea with an even bigger one of his own and I would return the favor. In the beginning he stated he wanted to run his own barbershop and while I was in college, he took over ownership of Unique and moved it to a newly renovated location.

When I first returned home after college, Otis was one of the first persons I turned to, as I was struggling with the idea of my football career being over. He helped me put my life into perspective. While others speculated about what might have happened had I went to another college, Otis explained, "God is incapable of making mistakes" and that every choice I made was for a reason, but it was up to me to figure out the purpose. I believed those words, so I started on a journey of reflection and through that journey grew a remarkable passion for the written word. Though Otis saw me as a phenomenal athlete, he embraced my transition from athlete to author. When the orders of my first book *When the Music Stops* returned from the printer, he took several copies and had them on display in the barbershop for purchase. We even discussed doing some other business ventures together in the future, but in the spring of 2007, Otis was killed in a fatal car accident. He was only 33 years old. During his abbreviated life here on earth, he often dedicated his time and money to helping me and countless others. That's why I dedicated this book to him.

Avoid Self-Inflicted Wounds

Two principle issues that continue to perpetuate the growth of poverty in black communities are teenage pregnancies and juvenile records. Avoiding these self-inflicted wounds will serve you well in your quest to rise above poverty. Teenage pregnancies and juvenile records are the results, not the actions. In order to avoid these pitfalls one must first address the actions.

It's tough being a young lady growing up in the hood—especially if you're attractive. From the moment you step outside guys circle like vultures. You have the older guys flashing money at you, hoping you take the bait and the younger guys trying to run script on you, hoping you don't recognize game.

Young ladies, if you want to rise above poverty, the best decision you could ever make is to practice abstinence. I know that almost sounds comical these days, but it is the truth. Immediately when you hear the word "abstinence" many people associate it with being religious. Ignoring the religious aspect of abstinence, let's examine it from a historical perspective. Statistics show that the highest black poverty rates occur in families headed by single women.

If you are currently a single teenage mother, it is not the end of the world; but please make certain that it is the end of your sexual activity until marriage. Having a second and third child out of wedlock will only decrease your chances of moving to a higher economic status.

Young men, if you want to rise above poverty avoid all criminal activity. Your best way out the hood is through securing a stable career. Felonies on your record will deter potential employers and it will be very difficult for you to secure employment.

If you own a gun, get rid of it! If you've considered selling drugs, forget about it! If you've shoplifted merchandise from a store, cut it out! 1 out of every 9 black men between the ages of 18-34 are incarcerated. It doesn't take much effort to fall into the trap. It's imperative that you understand how easy it is to go to jail and work diligently to avoid it.

Maximize Your Potential

One of the most overused and counterproductive phrases I hear from parents is, "I just want my child to do better than I did." I understand the sentiment, but the words send the wrong message. Your parents are basically giving verbal consent for you (the child) to underachieve. The danger in making a generalized statement like this—especially when you live in poverty—is that merely doing better than your parents may also land you in poverty. This is how generations of families remain impoverished. The bar is set too low.

If you were raised in a single-parent household where your mother only had a high school diploma and you attained a Bachelor's degree, you would be considered an overachiever. But if you were raised in a household where both your parents received PhDs and you attained a Bachelor's degree, you would be considered an underachiever.

If you know anything about high jumping, everyone starts at a different level based on past heights. The good ones don't waste their time or energy on lower level jumps. They wait until the bar is raised to their standards and then they begin jumping. Even after a winner has been declared, he or she will usually continue jumping in the attempt to set a new personal record. This is the epitome of setting the bar high and striving for new heights.

When I first began working in the corporate world, my mother was forty-eight years old. At twenty-four, my starting salary far exceeded her largest annual income, ever. Since I was the only person in my immediate family to graduate from college and now earning significantly more money than my mother, should I have been content with my status and stopped raising the bar? The message from parents to their children should be "maximize your potential!" Take your God given ability and talents and utilize them to the fullest extent. There are too many future lawyers and judges settling for court bailiff.

That was not meant to belittle anyone's profession; it was simply a memo to all the underachievers of the world to turn off the cruise control. Don't settle for being good, if you have the potential to be great. If you have the right attitude, no job should ever be beneath you or above you, only within arm's reach.

The time is over for excuses. Now is the time for examples. No more allowing circumstances in life to be a reason to fail. There is always a positive that can be found in every situation, even the worst kind. Due to my father's crack addiction, I never tried my hand at selling drugs. Had he not been addicted to crack, maybe I would have been able to disassociate selling drugs from poisoning the community. Maybe I would have been the dope boy selling drugs to some other kid's father.

Go To College!

There is more to success than just having a college degree, just as there is more to swimming than just holding your breath. Swimming requires technique and form, but if you don't first learn how to hold your breath, you will never be able to swim. If you have ever taken swimming classes, the first lesson you learned is how to hold your breath under water. It is one of the basic fundamentals of swimming. I view college in the same way with respects to starting a career. There are other professional skills that you must develop in order to have a successful career, but without a college degree it will be almost impossible to even begin the journey. College is absolutely necessary to rise above poverty. You should no longer consider college optional. It's mandatory.

When you graduated from the 8th grade, there was no debate whether or not you should attend high school. It was the natural next progression. High school was seen as a required step in the education process. College should be viewed the same way.

With more and more people attaining Master's and Doctorate degrees, undergraduate school has become the modern day high school. A Bachelor's degree, for all intents and purposes, is now equivalent to a high school diploma. Not in the sense that someone with a Bachelor's degree and someone with a high school diploma are equally as qualified, but in the sense that Bachelor degrees have been downgraded a level.

Relatively speaking, that makes a high school diploma now equivalent to an 8th grade diploma. Can you imagine walking into an interview for a job and handing your potential new employer a resume that states, your highest level of education is 8th grade? First, you probably wouldn't have made it to the interviewing process, but let's assume you did. How would you feel about your chances? Today, when you walk into interviews having only a high school diploma or GED (with no other trade school certification), you are sending the same message.

In this global economy, America struggles to compete with cheap foreign labor. The U.S. is slowly moving away from industrial manufacturing. Relatively good paying labor jobs that only require a high school diploma are becoming obsolete. They are being replaced by more service oriented jobs that require a Bachelor's degree or above.

It's like the value of money relative to inflation, as inflation goes up the value of a dollar declines. Over time that same dollar that used to buy you a bottled drink out of the vending machine, now will barely get you a small bag of chips. Each year costs increase—the price of raw materials, labor and transportation. Thus the end user, the consumer, sees an incremental increase in the price of his favorite soda or potato chips.

Likewise, each year thousands of students graduate from college, making the pool of qualified applicants more abundant. This consequently weakens the value of a Bachelor's degree in the corporate world. The same position you could have held ten years ago with a Bachelor's degree now requires an MBA.

Education and wealth have a direct correlation. It is not by coincidence that most rich people are well-educated, or that most people living in poverty are deficient in education. If your ultimate goal is to rise above poverty, higher education is the answer. In 2009 college graduates median income was 50% higher than young adults with a high school diploma (and double the income of high school dropouts).

If you join the work force right out of high school, initially you will have more money than your friends who chose to go to college; but long term you will be limited in how much money you can earn. That American Dream you hear talked about so casually won't be a reality for you. On the other hand, your friends will graduate college and within six years of working they will have earned more income than you. The longer they work the greater the gap will increase. As they receive promotions and build up their resume for strategic career moves, you will be stuck in the same dead end job with no potential for upward mobility.

Your education level and economic status have a direct correlation. With every degree that you earn, you make yourself more valuable in the career world. You have the opportunity to choose your employer and negotiate your salary; rather than take whatever work you can find and have your wages dictated by government regulations. In minimum wage jobs, there is usually little room for upward mobility, so the chances of working your way out of poverty are unlikely. The income you earn will provide just enough means to cover your cost of living. What about savings? Without the ability to put money away for the future, how will you ever save up enough money to purchase a home or save for retirement?

Establish Good Credit

Establishing a good credit history is essential in successfully defying the laws of poverty. Your credit score is a reflection of your credit history. Those three digits inform potential lenders if you are responsible enough to be extended a line of credit. Without good credit, you will need cash to pay for whatever you purchase. No credit is considered to be bad credit; therefore, it's important to use credit, but you have to be careful or you could get yourself into serious financial trouble.

First start by opening a checking account and learn how to manage it. Then open a savings account. There are still people walking around carrying money in their socks or at home under their mattress. Usually when you have money that is easily accessible, it spends quickly. Plus you can only store so much money under a mattress before it starts to feel lumpy and affect your sleep. Even if you don't have much money to commit to savings initially, open an account in anticipation of your future fortune. Once you've accumulated some savings, escalate to a credit card. Use your best judgment in making purchases. Only buy items that you need and can afford. Use part of your savings to pay off your balance in full every month to avoid finance charges. Replace the money you took from your savings and repeat the circle continuously.

Credit is any money, goods, or services you receive with expectation of future payment. Credit is something my mother never talked about. I was more familiar with layaway. With credit you receive your merchandise in advance with the understanding that you will make monthly payments until the balance is paid off. Layaway works differently. The store holds on to the merchandise (interest free) while you make monthly payments. Once you have paid the balance, only then will you receive your items.

Right around July every year, my mother would begin her Christmas shopping for me and my siblings. She would go to one of the big department stores and load her shopping cart full of shoes, clothes and other items. She would put it all on layaway and pay on it every month. It would take all the way until Christmas to pay off the balance. We were usually with my mother at the store when she put the items on layaway, but it would take so long that on Christmas Day, we were always surprised by the gifts under the tree.

If your parents never talked to you about credit, then like most kids, you learned from what you observed. Parents don't have to intentionally teach bad financial practices, because children learn through examples shown by their parents. If every time the phone rings with an 800 number on the other end your mother says, "Don't answer that! It's a bill collector." you are probably being taught the wrong way. If right before you walk into a family member's house your mother turns to you and says, "Remember we just got robbed" again, you are probably being taught the wrong way. If you were robbed, I think you would remember, just as you will remember all these instances when you get older and start creating debt. If you borrow money from family, pay them back. Don't make up stories, or avoid them in the streets. Better yet, don't borrow money (unless you absolutely must). It's a bad habit to develop.

Burn Your Race Card

Reach into your pocket or purse, pull out your wallet, remove your race card and burn it! It has no use. The expiration date has expired. Yes, slavery in America did occur. It is not an urban legend as some white Americans seem to view it. Black poverty is a direct result of slavery and the subsequent decades of racial inequality that followed it. By asking you to burn your race card, am I suggesting that we now live in a post-racial America? No! But playing the race card is a slippery slope that will hinder your progress out of poverty.

I acknowledge that racism is still alive. I've dealt with it personally. However, as a black man who has witnessed other blacks blame the white man for everything that has ever gone wrong in their lives, I am extremely cautious when labeling a person, situation, or remark as racist. I choose to weigh other options as the root cause. After I've exhausted all other possibilities, only then will I conclude that the issue was race related.

I'm certainly not asking you to turn a blind eye to racism; I'm asking you not to give it power. There are enough people in this world walking around committing crimes and hating people all in the name of racism. It has enough intrinsic power to fuel itself.

Racism concerns me, but I'm more concerned about you reaching your full potential. The race card is a self-handicapping crutch that will make your goals seem beyond the realm of possibility. You will convince yourself that it's too hard for a black person to be successful in this white man's world.

This topic could have been under the "become whole" section of this chapter, as playing the role of victim, or assuming that all white people are secretly out to oppress you will surely prevent you from being whole and experiencing the full scope of our freedom.

Broaden Your Horizon

If your only friends are black and impoverished, there is no doubt you will be prejudiced towards other races as well as blacks who are of a higher social class. In order to truly remove the racial barrier, you have to make a conscious effort. Think about it. If you live in an all-black community and attend an all-black school, church, etc., there are not many opportunities to build relationships with people of another race. Chances are most of your friends are black and live in the same neighborhood as you.

To breakdown the barrier you have to be deliberate. Whenever the opportunity presents itself, you have to reach out to people of another race in the attempt to develop a relationship. Find someone with a similar attitude as you, who is equally as interested in learning about other cultures, and enlighten one another.

Most of my growth as a person happened in college when I was able to interact with people from all different races, ethnicities and social classes. If you only associate with people of the same race and social class, your train of thought will remain constricted. Once you allow yourself to see the world from a broader perspective, it will give you a deeper understanding of human beings.

I'm not a fan of forging relationships, but I understand the importance of having friends of other races. Since living in an all-black community limits the opportunity, desperate times call for desperate measures.

Most people only have about one or two really close friends in life. Of which, both were probably childhood friends. As you get older, the difficulty with making new friends is that once you have your full complement of close friends, there is no motivation to reach out for more. Unless a void has been created by the absence of a friend due to geographic location or naturally growing apart, you usually keep all other friends at an arm's length. So if you live in an all-black community and you don't have any white, Asian, or Hispanic friends that doesn't necessarily make you a racist, it makes you normal.

4

"TALKIN' WHITE"

"Hi! How are you?" / "Ay! What it do?"

One of the easiest ways to determine whether or not you are suffering from an impoverished state of mind is to ask yourself, "Do I refer to blacks that use proper English and enunciate their words as 'talkin' white'?" There is no phrase more revealing than these two words. To say that another black person is "talkin' white" because he or she chooses to use correct grammar and enunciate their words when they speak, suggests to me that you grew up in an impoverished area where most African Americans used slang (or broken English) and you are unaware of the thousands of educated middle-class African Americans who use proper English on a daily basis.

There is no such thing as "talkin' white." Without being a mind reader, I know there are some of you sitting there thinking "Yeah Right!" but that's because you're taking my words out of context. I'm referring to correct grammar and vocabulary. You are including sound and pitch. I will concede that there is a difference in the way that black and white people sound. For instance, you can take two men, one black and one white, with the same level of education and have them read a sentence. There will be a distinct difference in their sound and pitch. Some blacks and whites get mistaken as the other race over the phone as a result of this distinction.

Now that I have clarified my definition of "talkin' white," I will repeat "There is no such thing!" The sooner we can dispel this myth the better. Then we can stop ignoring the truth regarding the use of proper English and illiteracy rates within impoverished black communities. The idea that someone can speak a color is quite idiotic. English is the national language of the United States and what most Americans speak (regardless of race). The English language has rules and guidelines concerning the written and verbal form of the language. There are proper and improper ways of speaking English, but there is no such thing as "talkin' white."

If "talkin' white" is using proper grammar and actual vocabulary, what exactly is "talkin' black?" Is it broken English and slang terms? If so, I must be biracial because depending on whom I'm having the conversation with—friend, family member, colleague, associate—I will fluctuate between proper and improper English. Dialects, tribal languages and slang alike are meant to draw distinctions—uniting one group and separating it from the masses. I use slang with friends to express kinship.

Though I'm guilty of using slang and improper English, I'm completely opposed to giving it a name (Ebonics) and referring to it as an English dialect or language. I also respectfully disagree with those who refer to Ebonics as African American Vernacular English (or Black English). I've read many arguments and linguistic analysis for why Ebonics should be viewed as a legitimate style of English (not just broken English) and treated with equal respect, but I'm simply not sold.

Referring to Ebonics as African American Vernacular English implies that all African Americans speak this language and only African Americans speak this language. Neither of which is true. It is not a matter of color, but rather a matter of education (or lack thereof). People who have not been formally educated on the use of proper grammar typically resort to a deviated form of English—I know because I was guilty of it.

For example, a sentence consists of a subject and a predicate. Without those key components, it's just a group of words strung together. The subject is what (or whom) the sentence is about. The predicate modifies the subject—informs you what the subject is doing. Within the predicate are typically a verb and an object. The verb describes the action and the object describes what (or whom) the verb is acting upon.

In the sentence "Deon is riding the bike," Deon is the subject and "riding the bike" is the predicate. Within the predicate, "riding" is the verb and "bike" is the object. Between the subject and predicate is the word "is." It acts as a linking verb to connect the subject and predicate. A fundamental understanding of these grammatical elements will help you speak and write clearer.

The use of double negatives is an example of common improper English. Words like no, not, nothing, nobody and nowhere are all negatives. The use of one in a sentence makes the statement negative. If used twice, the two negatives cancel each other and make a positive. For instance, if you were to say, "I don't have no money," what you are really telling the person is that you have money. The proper way to express that statement would be, "I do not have any money." Chances are they will probably keep asking you, but at least you will have finally told them what they needed to hear.

Another common grammatical mistake involves homonyms (words that are pronounced alike, but different in meaning); words like: bare and bear, pray and prey, hear and here, meat and meet, etc. The list goes on and on. Simple grammatical mistakes like this can make someone appear to be dumb or stupid, but it's just a matter of understanding the meaning and recognizing which word to use. The English language is not as easy to understand as one may think. It takes a conscious effort to understand and adopt its principles (not principals).

Finally, there are just examples of made-up words and words used out of context. A superlative is: of, relating to, or constituting the degree of grammatical comparison that denotes an extreme or unsurpassed level or extent. It is often indicated by the use of the suffix

-est. Let's say Arrin, Brian and Vincent all took a test. Arrin scored a 92%, Brian scored a 90% and Vincent scored an 87%. Arrin had the highest score of the three. There are some instances where the word used is already in its greatest form. Using the previous example, we could not say, "Vincent had the worstest score." "Worstest" is not a word. It would simply be worst, or the lowest.

A word used out of context, generally stated, is a word used in a sentence or phrase that does not match the meaning of the word. For example, if I said "I pacifically told you to park the car in the garage." The root word pacific means: tending to lessen conflict. The word I meant to use is "specifically" which means: having a special application, bearing, or reference.

Back in slavery, if anyone was caught teaching a colored person how to read, they were severely punished (if not killed). The inability of African Americans to speak standard English still lingers from this dark time in our history. If we continue to embrace "Ebonics" as it's own language, we are voluntarily perpetuating a sound that was forced upon us. If our ancestors were allowed to attend school like we are today, I am certain that they would have made every attempt to speak proper English. Since they were not allowed to go to school (and English was not there primary language), they were forced to learn the language by hearing it. Most of their days were spent out in the fields working with other slaves, so they learned how to articulate and pronounce words from listening to each other, which is equivalent to the blind leading the blind across the street.

As a child, I learned the correct way to pronounce words and proper sentence structure within the four walls of my classroom, but once outside the classroom, it was back to speaking the language of the streets. There was no repetition and follow-up on the knowledge learned at school. Since no one in my household spoke proper English, compounded with the fact that all my friends and people in my community used slang and broken English, it made it easy for my language flaws to go unnoticed.

In my neighborhood if you wanted food there was only one place to go, "Mary Dynast." It was a real hole-in-the-wall, but the place received steady business. Mary Dynast was famous for its cheeseburger and cheese steaks, but it was equally as famous for how greasy your paper bag would be by the time you made it home. If you didn't hold the bottom of the bag your food probably would have fell through. Over the years I probably went there hundreds of times, but it wasn't until years later, after the restaurant closed, that I found out its real name. A family member, who used to live in Robbins, came back to visit and she asked, "Is Mary's Diner still open?"

"Mary's Diner...Where is that?" I thought to myself. She went on to describe it and then it hit me, "Oh! You talkin' bout Mary Dynast?"

I went on to explain that it had closed down. Later when I was alone in my room I laughed at myself. I could not believe I never put two and two together to figure out that Mary Dynast was really named Mary's Diner. There was no sign in front of the diner to read the actual name, so I called it Mary Dynast because all my life I'd heard it called by that name. I never realized it was just lazy English and no one ever corrected me.

That's the difficult part about ignorance. You cannot recognize it until you gain the knowledge that will help you identify it. Ignorance keeps you at the mercy of other people relying on them to help you understand. You have to become informed.

To this day, I still struggle with pronouncing certain words correctly because of all the years of bad practice. In my mind, I know the right way to say the word, but somewhere between the point of it coming to mind and reaching my tongue, the proper pronunciation gets lost in the translation. Using proper English takes work, it requires repetition and close attention to detail.

I'm not suggesting you should walk around talking to your friends as if you're in a Shakespearian play "Wherefore art thou, Keisha?" I'm just suggesting that you learn correct English and then choose how you want to speak in any given environment.

What if I told you that the spelling of words is arbitrary? What if I also added that words—and definitions—are added to the English language (dictionaries) based on their popularity and frequency of (written) use? How would that make you feel? It's true. So when you look up the definition of black and white in a dictionary and realize that the word black is associated with negative adjectives like evil, sinister and wicked, and the word white is associated with positive adjectives like pure, flawless, unadulterated, it makes you wonder...

I'm fine with young black people being creative and innovative. Challenge the status quo. Create new words and spell them as you wish. Petition to get them implemented into the English language. However, there has to be some uniformity in order for the language to be universal, so stay true to the grammatical rules of the English language. For example, if you're going to create a new adjective make sure it modifies a noun, a pronoun, or another adjective.

In the attempt not to bore you, or turn this in to a proper grammar handbook, I'm not going to dive much deeper into the English language, but there are books you can purchase that can help you become more proficient. You can learn more about common grammatical errors like: lack of subject-verb agreement, sentence fragments, missing prepositions, dangling modifiers and comma splices. You must make an attempt to speak proper English. If you struggle with speaking proper English, then writing it will certainly be a challenge. The written form is much more formal and a lot less flexible.

Understanding Cultural Differences

Far too often people see color and want to paint scenarios black and white. But when a black kid grows up in an all-white community and in turn uses proper English, it's not because he's trying to be white. It's because of the make-up of the neighborhood and some of the other variables consistent with predominantly white neighborhoods, such as: parent's education level, quality of school districts, etc. These elements all factor into the equation. It's easy to take a complex issue and dummy it down by using something as general as race, but there is much more to the story. If the same black kid grew up in a predominantly white trailer park community, he would probably use broken English just as if he grew up in Crenshaw. It's a socioeconomic distinction not a racial one.

The way people talk has little to do with the color of their skin and everything to do with the zip code they live in. From the east coast, to the west coast, to down south, everyone sounds a little different. Not just in their accents, but in their regional dialect (diction)—words and phrases that we use to express ourselves. In the Midwest we say, "pop" to describe a soft drink, whereas people from the east coast say, "soda." In the south all soft drinks are referred to as a "coke." If you've ever been to New York and Atlanta, you know that the people in these cities talk considerably different. The slow southern drawl of the south is an extreme contrast to the quick pace sound of the east coast.

Just as people's speech changes from region to region and neighborhood to neighborhood, so do behaviors. If a black child grows up in a predominantly white middle-class neighborhood, that child's behavior patterns will mimic his environment. Culturally, that child will identify with the white race more than its own. Not because the child is an Uncle Tom, sellout, or white boy with a tan, it's because the child is a product of its environment. So what if a black girl from the valley uses like in a sentence three times…"Like, we like totally like did it!" or if a black guy, who grew up in a predominantly white neighborhood, prefers rock over hip hop. It doesn't make their skin any less black.

Color is an extremely generic way to group metals, let alone creatures as complex and multi-dimensional as human beings. Take platinum and white gold for instance. To the (untrained) naked eye, they both look the same. However, the two metals have different physical and chemical properties. These properties are what make the metals unique—not their color. Similarly, some blacks have looked at color as a personality trait rather than a race. They assume that all African Americans have to walk, talk and act the same. Those who do not fall into the stereotypical idea of "blackness" are ostracized from the community and labeled as sellouts.

I learned this best during my college years. College is packed full of different social groups and organizations, none more common than sororities and fraternities. They are good for making new friends, but they are usually extremely segregated. Thus, whenever I saw a black girl in an all-white sorority, I automatically concluded that she wanted to be white. But that is not necessarily the case. Due to everything I've stated earlier, often these black people feel more accepted by the white race than their own. Culturally, nothing about them reflects the tradition of the black community. They've been raised in an all-white neighborhood and socially identify more with the white community; therefore, they feel more comfortable being around whites.

One Fourth of July, while I was in college, I brought two of my teammates home with me for the holiday. One was an African American from Minnesota the other a Caucasian from Arizona; both were from an upper-middle class background. As we drove into my complex and they looked around at all the people standing out on the corner, they both seemed a little apprehensive. We visited for a while but didn't stay long. I could sense that they both felt out of their element, so I cut the stay short. I use this example just to draw home the point that it's not an issue of race. The discomfort they were feeling was from a socioeconomic standpoint. In their neighborhoods back home, I'm sure neither were used to people standing out on the corner, loud music playing from five different car stereos, people arguing, kids running around and police patrolling. This was unfamiliar to them. To me, it felt like home.

There are so many other elements that factor into the dimensions of a person—religion, geography, language and common beliefs. This is usually described as a person's culture. Each culture has its own rituals and unique characteristics that help further identify its members (i.e. music, food, clothing, etc). What makes a Jamaican a Jamaican? What makes a Hawaiian a Hawaiian? What makes a Jew a Jew? What makes an Amish person Amish? What makes an Igbo an Igbo? The answer is, "A host of different attributes." Some make reference to geographic locations, others religious beliefs or ethnic groups. It really comes down to how you identify yourself. Some people identify with race or gender; others identify more with economic status or religion.

Complying vs. Conforming

To understand why certain stereotypes exist about the black culture, you must first ask the question, "How is black culture portrayed in the media?" When depicting the black community on television through sitcoms, movies, reality shows and rap videos, directors choose to portray the hood. They ignore the existence of the countless African Americans living outside the hood. That's why "blackness" takes on this stereotypical ideology of being underprivileged, over-sexualized, scholastically ignorant, street savvy, rough and rugged; yet these characteristics have little to do with being black and more to do with being a part of the underworld.

Some African Americans recognize they are black but choose not to embrace their blackness because they see what it means to be a stereotypical black and since they do not fit the description they don't truly identify with the race. If you don't fully understand what I'm referring to when I say "stereotypical black," buy tickets to see your favorite black stand-up comedian. Black comedy shows are the best examples of racial stereotyping. If you've ever watched one you know exactly what I'm talking about. It's usually a compare and contrast type of scenario.

"When white people go to the movies they purchase their tickets then stand in line at the concession stand to procure refreshments; but when we (blacks) go to the movies, black women find the biggest purse in their closet and stuff it to the brim. They walk in with their knockoff

Dooney & Bourke trash bag over their shoulder talkin' 'bout 'which way is theater 1?' Anything that won't fit in their purse, us guys strap to our chest and walk in looking like the abominable snowman."

I'm not suggesting there is no truth to these jokes. However, does this truly represent all black people or just those who are poor and cannot afford to pay for the overpriced refreshments at movie concession stands? Are there no poor white people that approach going to the movies the same way?

Being black is what you are, not who you are. Don't ever let anyone try to force you into a box because of your skin color. Be who you are! Love yourself! Embrace all that makes you unique. Never let anyone convince you that you need to act a certain way to be considered "black." African Americans (like any other race) are multi-dimensional, multi-faceted people.

On the other hand, don't ever believe you need to have a mainstream look to get ahead. By "look" I mean the way you wear your hair, or your style of clothes. Guys, rock your dreads. Ladies, go natural. Wear your ethnic jewelry and clothes, if you choose. The goal is not to eliminate stereotypes and racism by eliminating the race. For far too long, minorities have had to conform to the white Anglo-Saxon way of life. Why? People should be able to express their ethnic roots (hairstyle, clothing, etc.) freely without feeling like they will have to suffer consequences.

Too much emphasis is put on the way young people dress. Every generation has its "what was I thinking" era, when we look back at old photo albums and scratch our heads wondering about our style of clothing. This generation is no different. People should be able to express themselves through their dress and not feel like they have to conform to a standard.

That being said, fashion is a choice. You wake up every day and make a conscious decision about what to wear. Your clothes are a representation of self. The way you dress should reflect the amount of respect you have and demand for yourself. It's all about maintaining a certain level of decency.

If a woman approaches you wearing nothing but a miniskirt, fishnets and a see-through halter top, would you be wrong for assuming she is a woman of the night? If a man approached you wearing make-up, long fingernails and carrying a purse, would you be wrong for concluding he is a transvestite? We prejudge based on appearances every day. The image we present to the world is what we are judged by, and rightfully so. We make a conscious decision on how we dress, so that speaks volumes about the mind frame of people who choose to dress in certain ways.

If you dress like a gangsta or a thug and you wonder why people mistake you for one, take a good look in the mirror. Besides family, classmates, co-workers, or someone that has reoccurring interactions with you, people do not have the luxury of knowing who you are on the inside; therefore you must project your inner-self outward.

Knowledge vs. Intelligence

My first day of kindergarten, I walked eagerly into class with my mother. The teacher came over and introduced herself.

"Hello, my name is Mrs. Sandover."

"Hi," I said, as she guided me over to where the rest of the students were sitting.

My twin cousins were starting kindergarten also, but they were not as enthused as I, so my mother went with my aunt to help calm them down. Shortly after my mother left, Mrs. Sandover started going over all the supplies we would need for class. As she went down the list, I looked in my book bag to make sure I had everything.

"Scissors?"

"Check!"

"Glue?"

"Check!"

"Crayons?"

"Check!"

"Markers..." I didn't have markers, so I raised my hand.

"Those of you who do not have markers need to get some." she said.

I didn't realize she meant to acquire markers at a later date. My young mind interpreted that as meaning "go right now." I convinced another girl in the class to come with me and we walked out the door.

We both lived in the projects. They were about a five minute walk from the school. When I got home, I walked in the door and immediately my grandmother said, "What you doin' home?" I explained to her that I needed markers for school and that the teacher sent me home. I was so convincing that my grandmother believed my story; in fact she started helping me search for markers around the house. Meanwhile back at the school my mother had returned to my classroom only to find out that her five year old son was missing.

I collected all the markers I could find and with my classmate I headed back to the school. When we walked back into the classroom, I'm not sure who was happier to see us, my mother or Mrs. Sandover. My mother looked relieved, but she just kept saying, "Don't ever leave the room without telling someone. Don't ever leave the room without telling someone." I explained to her that I was just trying to be a good student.

I took the first day of kindergarten so seriously because my mother instilled the importance of education in me at a very early age. Over the years, she (accompanied by her leather belt) let it be known that bad grades were unacceptable in our household.

If your parents never took you to McDonalds as a child, would you have cried every time you drove past and they didn't stop to get you a Happy Meal? No! You would've never noticed, but they took you occasionally and you associated McDonalds with Happy Meals and you wanted your toy. Your parents created your craving for Happy Meals by first introducing them to you.

Along with your love for Happy Meals, your parents should have instilled a love for learning. Granted, school plays a huge part in providing a child with an education, but home is where the primary education takes place and parents must first create and cultivate the thirst for knowledge. You don't have to be a genius to enjoy learning about foreign topics. But you do have to seek knowledge.

Over time I've learned the difference between "intelligence" and "knowledge." I never thought of the two words as synonyms, or used them in a sentence interchangeably, but I subconsciously viewed them as equal. Learning the difference between the two changed my perspective forever.

Intelligence refers to brainpower, mind capacity, or aptitude, while knowledge merely measures the level of a person's mental storage. Let's say your brain was a box and the items you place inside the box represent knowledge. The bigger the box the greater capacity you have to store knowledge. Some people are born with slightly bigger boxes than others. There are some who were born with supersized storage boxes; these are the people we refer to as geniuses.

The word genius refers to someone with extreme intelligence or mind capacity. Geniuses are born not made. Every human being is born with a certain IQ level which is arguably impossible to enhance. And it's only through continuous drug and alcohol abuse, a rare health condition, or severe head trauma that IQ levels can deteriorate.

Being knowledgeable does not make you smart. Being smart makes you smart. Being knowledgeable is important, but is not a measurement of intelligence. Being knowledgeable speaks to the knowledge of a person, which can be learned, rather than the core competency of a human being. That is why I'm vehemently opposed to standardized tests like the SAT and ACT. I believe they lean too much on the knowledge of a person rather than pure intellect. I realize a student must have a basic understanding of the fundamentals of Math, Science and English in order to survive in a college environment, but beyond that the test should measure a student's potential (i.e. capacity to learn). It should be unbiased, in which people from all walks of life are measured on an equal playing field. The way to accomplish this is to make the test more abstract than real. There should be a verbal component of the test. For instance, create a list of abstract words and ask the student to pronounce them. Give him a list of words to remember and keep adding words, one at a time, until they can't remember them all. Draw a picture with a hodge-podge of different elements and have the student make a storyline out of it. Conduct the test over the course of a week, so you measure the student's ability to learn and retain knowledge.

Referring back to the nature vs. nurture argument, intelligence is an attribute that a person is born with naturally; whereas knowledge is acquired and this acquisition is highly subject to an individual's surroundings. Some people are knowledgeable about significant topics; others fill their brain with trivial information—knowledge that really has no use outside of game nights. This type of knowledge comes in handy during rounds of Taboo, Trivial Pursuit and Catch Phrases, but that's about it.

The vast majority of my college classmates attended private institutes for high school, where their yearly tuition ranged anywhere from $15K-$20K. For the sake of their parent's investment, I would hope they were exposed to more curriculum than I was at a public high school—making them more knowledgeable.

We are all ignorant. Nobody knows everything about every topic, but when you're lacking the fundamental knowledge necessary to succeed in this country, you can only help yourself by gaining knowledge.

Hopefully none of you have experienced cancer treatment at your young age, but if you have, you know that as a patient you become as knowledgeable about cancer (and the treatment of it) as the doctor. Why? Because cancer is a matter of life and death and the severity of it demands your undivided attention. If you could only look at foundational knowledge in terms of life or death, you would understand its importance.

It's an uncertain world out there for people who don't have the basic operational understanding of computers or the internet. There is a strong push to make America a more paperless society, from banking institutions to the way we receive our daily news. If you lack the knowledge to navigate the system, you will be at an extreme disadvantage. The only solution is to get informed.

As a freshman in college, I sat in class listening to the professor give instructions for our research papers.

"Papers must be between 15-20 pages. I want them double-spaced, 12 point font, Times New Roman. In regards to citing, you can use MLA or APA."

I thought to myself, "I would choose one, if I knew what the heck MLA or APA meant."

I looked around the room at the faces of my classmates hoping to find someone who shared my sentiments, but everyone looked perfectly fine with the instructions.

Too embarrassed to ask the simple question "What do you mean by MLA and APA?" I left class and immediately went to the campus bookstore. I found a book on the topic. It explained that MLA and APA were different formats to citing a paper where references are used to protect the author of the paper from plagiarizing (or taking credit for someone else's original thoughts). I purchased the book and over the next couple of months, I taught myself how to properly cite a paper.

There are several other examples of situations where I had to teach myself on the fly, when I lagged behind the rest of the student body. I started second guessing my decision to attend Northwestern, but quitting was never an option. The competitor in me was not willing to give up without a fight. Once I realized that I was just as intelligent as most of my classmates, only I was lacking the level of knowledge, I overcame my inferiority complex. I opened up book after book and tried to expand my knowledge across an array of topics.

Theory of Multiple Intelligences

This theory was introduced by psychologist, Howard Gardner (professor at Harvard University) in the early 80s. His theory challenged the traditional method of measuring intelligence, suggesting that it did not encompass the full capacity of human ability. Our minds have a unique way of learning and processing knowledge based on the way we are intellectually wired. The theory of multiple intelligences argues that there are seven basic types of intelligences: spatial, linguistic, logical-mathematical, bodily-kinesthetic, musical, interpersonal and intrapersonal.

Someone with a high aptitude for spatial intelligence can visualize conceptually without having everything laid out in front of them. These types of people make good designers, architects and interior decorators, but not necessarily great dancers. That requires a high aptitude for bodily-kinesthetic intelligence, which may not be present. To take someone who has a high aptitude for musical intelligence and attempt to measure their intellect with complex mathematical problems is futile. Albert Einstein, one of the forefathers of innovative thought, concluded that, "Everybody is a genius. But if you judge a fish by its ability to climb a tree, it will live its whole life believing that it is stupid."

Human beings are very complex creatures with very unique qualities; therefore, I tend to agree with Einstein and Dr. Gardner's theory. Beethoven was deaf, yet he was a master composer. That suggests to me that human beings are born with certain intellectual predispositions. Just because someone who was born with mathematical intelligence can solve for x better than a poet with more linguistic intelligences does not mean that person is more intelligent overall than the poet.

People like to use the term "dumb jock" to demean athletes with superior athletic ability. Often the label has little to do with their actual IQ and more to do with their athletic prowess. People with extreme intellectual ability (geniuses) were born with that gift. They did nothing more to receive their gift than an athlete with extreme physical talent. We are all gifted; just in different ways.

5

PRO-BLACK/ANTI-NIGGA

"Too many young folk have addiction to superficial things and not enough
conviction for the substantial things like justice, truth and love."
—Cornel West

There was a time in our history when being black symbolized beauty,
dignity and power; the beauty of black families living in unity, the dignity of self-worth and the power to overcome injustice. In the face of
adversity, we began a movement—one that would require great sacrifice. All based on the promise of a better future. Some gave their lives
for the cause, but in the process a new ideology was birthed, a belief
that ignited black pride in a way that had never been seen before. It
would forever change the way African Americans viewed themselves
and become widely known as the Black Power Movement.

Some viewed the Black Power Movement as racial division, because it promoted separatism, but blacks and whites were already
segregated. This was just an attempt to provide blacks a solution to
segregation, by having them control what was within their power. The
Black Power Movement focused on strengthening the black community through political involvement, black entrepreneurship, education
and overall black progress.

Not all positives came out of the Black Power Movement, but one
would be hard-pressed to argue that it didn't fundamentally change
blacks' perception of their own race. African Americans were once
said to be "a race with no identity" because we were stripped from
our African roots and planted in American soil as slaves. The African

American race itself originated in slavery. Prior to coming to America, we were simply Africans. While the first generation of African slaves were still in tune with the African culture—rituals, spirituality, norms—350 years later all aspects of African culture had been extracted and supplanted by African American slave culture—leaving us with no identity other than slavery.

Through the Black Power Movement, we were able to find ourselves. Instead of being embarrassed of our dark past, we began to celebrate our heritage. There was a renewed sense of self-worth and pride in our culture that had been lost over hundreds of years of slavery. Being black no longer brought about a feeling of despair; it was an honor and privilege to be an African American. It made you a part of the Black Power Movement.

Bridging the Gap

We were bred to endure
And suffer beyond the shores of our hearts
Into the deep rivers of our souls
For we are the descendants of courageous and extraordinary people
Slaves of their day, but not of their mind
Ignorant in comparison to most
Yet wisdom well beyond their time

We stand proud today
Not in arrogance but in faith
Knowing that we've overcome slavery
And stood firm against social inequities

We push forward with the promise of a better tomorrow
As for today, we give thanks and pray through our sorrows
These are the qualities deeply rooted within
Beyond our caramel complexion or dark brown skin
We are intelligent...we are resilient...we are strong...we are
CHAMPIONS!

There is a painfully obvious disconnect between the black communities of today and that of those back in the 50s and 60s. Back then, black people understood the struggle, as African Americans were still fighting to overcome segregation. Now, as more than forty years has passed since the Civil Rights Act of 1964, it appears the knowledge of our history has been lost upon the new generation. Either schools are not teaching black history, or parents and grandparents have stopped passing down their family history.

I remember as a child, my grandmother would share stories about her childhood. Though I was too young to appreciate the knowledge that was being passed on to me, I enjoyed the narration. It felt like story time at school. As I got older and learned more about the history of blacks in America, I was able to put these stories into context. It helped me better understand my family history and how we ended up living in a housing project for over 40 years.

Granny was born in Clarksdale, Mississippi in the late 1920s—60 years after slavery was legally abolished. She was the third youngest of twelve children (two siblings died from Tuberculosis, one died as a baby and another was stillborn). Their family was sharecroppers (Sharecroppers were tenant farmers who worked the land in return for food, shelter and an agreed share of the value of the crop).

Sharecropping became popular post-Civil War, after the Thirteenth Amendment was ratified abolishing slavery. Plantation owners became desperate for workers, but could not afford to pay wages. Legally, all slaves were free at this point, so forced labor was outlawed; but with no money, or means of making any, former slaves were forced into the sharecropping system.

Sharecropping was simply slavery by another name. Throughout her childhood Granny and her family lived on several plantations. At the end of the year, when it was time for them to be compensated for their work, the landowner would find reason not to pay. He would accuse them of costing him money for broken tools, or they would be penalized for not reaching a certain amount of acres. The family would then cut their ties and move to another plantation, only to deal with the same situation by year's end.

In the sixth grade, Granny was forced to drop out of school and join her family in the field. Her father died of a heart attack, so there became more work than there were hands. The rest of her childhood was spent picking cotton with her siblings from sunrise to sunset.

The death of her father—and the general quality of life for a sharecropper—took its toll on Granny's mother. She was never the same after he passed. Overtime, she became sick and eventually suffered a nervous breakdown. After her mother became mentally ill, Granny and her siblings decided to move north, in search of a better life; but it wasn't that simple. They were still working as sharecroppers, so they couldn't just pack up and leave. Apparently, they were still "in debt" to the landowner. If they attempted to leave, he would have tried to stop them; so they put together a plan to sneak away in the middle of the night. They packed everything they could fit into their knapsacks, then took the rest of their belongings and started a bonfire. They were terrified of being caught, so they made certain not to leave a trace.

They waited until the night was silent and then set out on their journey. They walked for miles and as they approached town, they spotted Old Man Smith, who would have surely turned them in, so they ran and hid underneath a viaduct until the coast was clear. They made it into town and purchased one-way train tickets north to Chicago. This was in 1942 during The Second Great Migration, where millions of southern African Americans moved north, to escape extreme racism and find employment.

They settled in a small village outside of Chicago called Robbins. Though an underdeveloped neighborhood, Robbins was recognized as a progressive African American community. It was later deemed the "Harlem of the Midwest" for such contributions as being the fifth oldest African American incorporated municipality in the United States and for having the first black owned and operated airport in the country—Robbins Airport.

At eighteen years of age and with only a six grade education, Granny was limited in the type of jobs she was qualified to work. She found a job working at a hat factory (Universal Hat & Cap MFG.) and would remain there for over thirty years, until the company went out of business.

In the early 60s, Cook County built a low-income public housing project in Robbins. Granny was now a single-mother raising four children and struggling to make ends meet, so she moved into the project shortly after it was built.

Over a forty-year span she watched the degradation of Robbins, as it transformed from a progressive black ghetto to a violent, drug-infested hood. Like other black communities, Robbins' transformation can be attributed to a variety of issues.

Since slavery the majority of black communities have been poor, but they were not dangerous. Black families lived peacefully in poverty. Prior to the 1970s, during the struggle for civil rights, violent crimes in the black community were a result of white on black hate crimes. It was not until the outbreak of heroin (post-Vietnam) and organized gang activity in the mid-70s that black-on-black crimes became prevalent. Couple that with the election of Ronald Reagan (whose Reaganomics negatively impacted the black community), the crash of the steel industry in the 80s and subsequent crack epidemic and you've created a dangerous cocktail of drugs, gangs and unemployment that crippled a black community on the rise. From 1959 to 1969, the black poverty rate went from 55.1% to 32.2%. However, from 1969 to 1993 the black poverty rate remained virtually flat. Once you prevent people from being able to earn an honest living, they resort to less constructive methods of supporting themselves. This is how peaceful black ghettos became treacherous black hoods! Once gangsta rap hit the scene in the early 90s and became marketable, this whole celebration of the hood, "I'm a thug" phenomenon emerged.

Coming from the South, where she lived on a plantation in a

one-room shack, the projects represented advancement for Granny; they were modern, all the utilities functioned properly and the rent was affordable. The change in the environment was gradual enough that she barely noticed. Granny was too busy raising four kids on her own. Though she left this earth without leaving behind any monetary inheritance, her sacrifice, as a mother—giving her children a stable home and strong morals and values—built a legacy of strong parental standards that was passed down to my mother. Standards I hope to one day pass on to my daughter.

How I wish Granny could have found a way to move the family out of the projects; regardless, I consider her a success. She was born in a different era where opportunities to advance were not readily available. Success is not measured by what you have, but rather by what you have overcome. Knowing the hardship Granny had to face and the sacrifices that she made for her family, how could I consider her anything less? More importantly, how could I not honor her legacy by doing everything in my power to maximize my potential?

What Does It Mean to be Black?

What does it mean to be black in America? It depends on who's answering the question. The black experience varies from person to person, city to city, social class to social class; but what is true of all blacks from all cities and social classes is that the color of your skin predisposes you to racial profiling, under-employment, higher incarceration rates, fewer resources, less opportunities and more adversity.

Since this country's inception we as descendants of African slaves, have endured a long history of civil injustice and inequality. As a race, we have been victorious in our quest for equality. This has added fuel to our fire and given us strength for the fight. In our relentless pursuit we have reached many milestones on our journey which have changed African American culture forever.

After centuries of struggling for equality, we find ourselves in a position to reach prosperity. An African American today can be born into poverty, work hard, go to college, graduate and start a lucrative career, but that person must be prepared to face some adversity. And when the opportunity presents itself you must be ready to seize the moment because opportunities for African Americans remain constricted.

There are many African Americans and other races who deny the reality of being black in America; but the numbers don't lie. We are the same race of people who saw the first African American president voted into office—after 43 straight Caucasian presidents. We are the same race of people that represent only six CEOs of the Fortune 500 companies in 2012 (13 total in the 57-year history of the Fortune 500). We are the same race of people that make-up the majority of the National Football League, but have yet to realize its first black majority owner. We are the same race of people that find ourselves locked behind bars at a rate that is unparallel to any other race. We are the same race of people who from 1984 to 2007 experienced the wealth gap between whites and blacks increase fourfold from $20,000 to $95,000. These are the harsh realities that unite us together. This is what it means to be black in America. It doesn't matter if you are running for president or running from the police. These statistics suggest that there is a great disparity between blacks and whites in America.

Black Entrepreneurship

Back in the early 1900s, a small neighborhood in Tulsa Oklahoma named Greenwood became famous for its thriving black-owned businesses. Due to segregation laws, blacks were not permitted to patronize any white establishments. This forced blacks to create their own clothing stores, restaurants, schools, newspapers and hotels. The Greenwood businesses became so successful that the neighborhood earned the nickname "Black Wall Street." Greenwood continued to enjoy unprecedented success until the Tulsa Race Riot of 1921. Much of the Greenwood neighborhood was destroyed, but Greenwood citizens rebuilt the community. What ultimately ruined the Greenwood community was desegregation. Once blacks were no longer forced to live in black communities or patronize black businesses, they took their money and spent it at white-owned businesses which ultimately crippled the Greenwood economy.

African Americans have to continue to push for entrepreneurship. More black-owned and supported businesses within black communities are necessary for the growth of the community. Continuing to take your money outside of the community to buy food, clothes, and household goods will keep your community impoverished.

First, there has to be established businesses within the community to buy food, clothes, etc. That means someone must have the courage to step out and attempt to become an entrepreneur. It might start off as something small that you do from your house that grows into something much greater, but you have to start somewhere.

It might be a family affair; a situation where the entire family invests some money into the business to get it started. Who knows how the business will become established, but there is a major need for more black owned business within the black community. That goes for all other minority communities as well, but other minorities seemed to have already figured out the secret.

When I'm in the mood for some good Chinese food, I usually go to Chinatown. When I'm there, it always amazes me how many Chinese owned and operated restaurants there are within a stones throw of each other. What's even more amazing is how well they appear to get along—despite the competitive aspect of their relationship. The Chinese definitely have the blueprint when it comes to entrepreneurship and building up one's own community.

Why can't blacks live, work and own businesses together in one community without turmoil? We can—as proven by Black Wall Street! But there are some challenging dynamics in the black community that hinder the growth of more communities like Black Wall Street. I date these issues back to slavery. Even then there were social classes. There were the upper-class house slaves and then there were the lower-class field slaves. White slave masters turned slaves against one another. They knew slaves outnumbered slave masters, so they needed allies on the inside to protect against a coup.

Slave masters gave the house slaves slight preferential treatment to make them feel like they were a part of the slave master's family; then used their loyalty to turn them against their fellow slaves.

There were five or six other families that lived on the plantation while my grandmother and her family were sharecroppers. I asked her if she had many friends in the other families and her response was a quick, "No!"

She went on to say, "We didn't associate with other families." I was curious as to why?

She explained "They thought that they were better than us."

This issue of division within the African American community is not a new phenomenon. Its presence is deeply woven in the fabric of our history.

Hood Rich

You've heard the notion that, "You can take a person out of the hood, but you can't take the hood out of a person." This phrase is usually used as a negative statement to denote lack of class (etiquette) by someone who has moved from a deprived socioeconomic status to one more privileged. I disagree with this statement. I agree that money alone cannot change a person, but I disagree with the notion that you can't take the hood out of a person. Anyone, regardless of the environment, can change the non-innate aspects of their character (if they so choose).

There is a process, with necessary steps, that needs to take place in order to physically and mentally remove yourself from the hood—a reconditioning of the mind. That's why people who become rich overnight struggle with overcoming their impoverished state of mind, because they have skipped the necessary steps essential to rising above poverty. It takes a tremendous amount of effort and sacrifice to rise above poverty. Once you've weathered the storm and come out victorious, you've grown as a person and developed certain characteristics that will better equip you to handle wealth.

People who win the lottery, professional athletes and other overnight millionaires who were raised in poverty alike are prime examples of this phenomenon (especially those who are young). Being young and having millions of dollars without the opportunity to grow and mature can be a gift as well as a curse. With enough money to do whatever you want, whenever you want, there is no incentive to change.

As a young athlete fresh out of the hood, if there was a rule that allowed football players to enter the NFL draft directly out of high school, my name would have been first on the list. If I was taken by a team, the first thing I would have done is bought a new car and put everything I could fit on it (from sounds, rims, tint, hydraulics, candy paint, Lamborghini doors, Louis Vuitton interior, etc.). I was young then and used to not having money, so it would have shown. After years of working on books, starting a company and all the effort and sacrifice that came along with both, I have a much greater respect for money. I can safely say that in my new found wealth, I will not be driving around in a car like the one described above.

If you're living in poverty right now, embrace it. Don't ever feel ashamed of your humble beginnings. Be proud of where you're from. Your background helped make you who you are today. However, you will need to part ways with some of the foolish and immature thoughts of your past—money is not a cure.

The Art of Being a Nigga

Generally speaking I'm a pretty laid back person. I'm typically not bothered by many things, but if there is one thing I cannot stomach… one thing that will send my blood pressure through the roof, it's an African American acting or behaving like a nigga. Yes, I said NIGGA!

Though I despise the word "nigger," I believe it is helpful to analyze its meaning in order to better understand the history of the word and the modern day term that derived from that history.

The origin of the word "nigger," as an ethnic slur, can be dated back as early as the nineteenth century. The word itself is merely an English variant of the Latin word *niger* which literally means "black." The negative connotation that surrounds the word today was created by the derogatory nature in which it was used by white Americans throughout slavery and the Civil Rights era.

During slavery, African Americans had no rights. They were considered to be property, except for distribution of taxes and other government affairs, where slaves were then counted as three-fifths of a white man. Slaves could not own land, earn wages, or vote. They were denied clothes, food and other bare necessities, not to mention the incredible physical abuse they endured. Blacks were taught to believe that they were an inferior race undeserving of being equal to their white counterpart (some black people are still struggling to get past this belief). Above all heinous acts, the most criminal was denying slaves the right to an education. The intent of white slave owners was to permanently keep African Americans in a powerless position. They understood the strength of knowledge and recognized that allowing slaves to become educated would be to white slave owners own detriment.

Theoretically speaking, based on what we know about slavery and the perception of slaves by white slave owners, the term "nigger" was generically used to describe a group of people who were "untamed, uneducated and immoral." Though I disagree with their assessment and use of the word "nigger" altogether, this uncovers the intended meaning of the term.

"Nigger" may have originated back in slavery and been meant as a derogatory word aimed at African American slaves, but in today's society, the "-er" has been replaced by an "a" and the word "nigga" takes on a much broader meaning. Though often used throughout the African American community, "nigga" does not only refer to a person of color. A "nigga" can be of any race, gender or ethnicity. Much like being a thug or a gangsta, being a "nigga" is a mentality. It's a way of thinking and an approach to life.

In its simplest form, a "nigga" refers to anyone who behaves like they are untamed, uneducated and immoral. People you cross paths with who carry themselves like they belong in a zoo rather than in society; men that act like vultures (scavengers) and women who behave like hyenas.

One summer night on the west side of Chicago, I was driving home from work and I passed a group of black people standing on the block drinking and listening to music. As I drove up, I saw a young lady in the street dancing wild and crazy. As I got closer to the crowd, I could hear her shouting, "Heeeey! Turn dat sh*t up! Dat's my sh*t!" as she continued to dance. Then right as I crossed her path, she leaped on the hood of a car and starts dancing on all fours with her skirt in the air and her thong making everyone's acquaintance. Not to pass judgment on the young lady, but that is the epitome of "nigga" behavior— someone acting untamed, uneducated and immoral. As ridiculous as this story sounds, I've witnessed these occurrences more often than I'd like to admit.

Similar to how using improper English (Ebonics) is embracing a sound that was forced upon us, behaving in an unruly manner that perpetuates the stigma of an African American as a nigger is unacceptable. We have a social responsibility to ensure that our actions are helping to progress the African American race.

The Need for a Black Agenda

When you have a race of people who were forced into slavery and as a result are disproportionately poor, we must fight to make sure there are ample opportunities for blacks to rise above poverty—even if that requires a black agenda, affirmative action, racial quotas, or a Rooney Rule (NFL). We must fight to maintain what was gained during the Civil Rights Movement and build on the momentum. We must protect the integrity of the American Dream and ensure that it is attainable for all African Americans—regardless of social class. Our job as young black leaders of tomorrow is to eliminate all impedances. Education is the door to unlimited possibilities. Thus, affordable education is crucial to the advancement of the African American race. No African American accepted to a top university should have to be in debt up to their neck or choose not to attend the university. As reparations for slavery, there should be government subsidies in place to assist with college tuition—dub it the "40 acres and a mule" scholarship.

Before we can focus our attention outward, we have to first take a long look in the mirror and realize that there are significant internal issues we are facing as a race that desperately need to be addressed. Despite all the round table discussions and debates over the need for a black agenda, there is no agenda imaginable that will help advance the race greater than black people themselves. In fact, unless the mindsets of the people change, no agenda will be able to right the ship. Change has to occur at the grassroots level; one person at a time, one family at a time, one community at a time.

Granted, poor black people are in a state of emergency when it comes to unavailable health care, unavailable child care and under-funded schools. The notion that somehow more money from the government for childcare and education will help strengthen the black community—where teenage pregnancies continue to spiral out of control and high school dropout rates are in double digits and growing—sounds counterintuitive. We would only be pacifying the situation while the real issue remains unaddressed.

That said, the plight of poor African Americans has always been an afterthought when developing the American agenda. That's why in most major inner-cities, we have a failing public school system that is altering the career trajectory of poor minority students. The lack of resources, funding, good teachers, and the increasing disparity between public and private, urban and suburban schools perpetuates poverty through generations.

The issues that poor blacks face have played second fiddle to the white majority, but that doesn't have to be the case. There are 41 million African Americans in America. One voice alone might not move a stone, but 41 million in unison will tear down a wall. I'm not suggesting that we all come together to sing Kumbaya and pretend that the African American race is harmonious, because it's not. We come from different social classes and backgrounds with a vast array of political views, but one thing we all can agree on is that equality still eludes us. We may argue over different approaches, but we all share the common goal. To reach that goal African Americans must be more unified. We have to canvass the community and make sure the interest of the black majority is being protected. We have to put pressure on our elected officials to represent our needs. We have to do research on candidates and make ourselves knowledgeable voters. We have to turn out at off-year elections and exercise our right to representation. We need more African Americans to run for office. We need more men and women of color (and integrity) at the state and local level. This is how we make issues in the black community gain more attention.

Regardless of individual election outcomes, you have to trust that the system works. It is absolutely flawed, but if you get to the point where you lose faith in it, you will stop trying. The quest for equality is a long journey, but by taking one step at a time we can and will arrive at our destination. It won't be because we all became rappers and turned the country into one big hood. It will be due to the diligence of young people like you who broke through poverty and achieved a better life for their family.

To help put things into proper perspective let me explain what I mean by "equality." The United States has a population of roughly

311 million people. African Americans make up 13.1% of the population (or 41 million). White (non-Hispanic) Americans make up 63.4% (or 197 million). In a country where blacks only make up 13.1% of the population, it would be foolish to think that blacks would ever match white Americans 1:1 in the corporate world, colleges, or congress. To have 250 African American CEOs in the Fortune 500 is neither realistic nor reflective of equality for all. Conversely, there is no reason why African Americans should make up 38% of the prison population while only accounting for 13.1% of the overall population. Contrary to how blacks are portrayed in the media, this is not due to the uncivilized nature of the African American race. This is in part a result of bias in the judicial system. The disparity in time served for crack possession (more commonly distributed in the black community) versus the powder form of cocaine (a more affluent party drug in the white community) is significantly greater. Those convicted of crack possession received 50% more jail time.

Ultimately, equality for blacks will be accomplished when we can represent 13.1% population throughout all facets of American culture (Capitol Hill or Rikers Island). That should be the focus and chief objective.

YES WE CAN!

During the writing of this book, I decided to take a hiatus as our nation slowly approached the 2008 Presidential Election—where for the first time an African American had a strong chance of winning. I stopped writing because I knew if what I was hoping for manifested before our eyes; it would change the reflection of this book and more importantly of this country forever. Not only because Barack Obama is a black man, but because he is a minority. In a country where the majority has ruled for so long, this would be a monumental change in America's DNA. America would now resemble more closely the country she was born to be. Expressed so eloquently by Thomas Jefferson, one of

America's forefathers, in the Declaration of Independence, "We hold these truths to be self-evident that all men are created equal..."

The one misconception about Barack Obama becoming president is the idea that we (African Americans) somehow, "beat out" the white race. There were plenty Caucasian Americans who were a part of Barack Obama's campaign team, not to mention the millions of other white people who voted for him. They did so because they believed in "change," not reverse discrimination. Did I feel this country was well overdue for an African American president...YES! For that reason I am very proud, but by no means do I feel like we (African Americans) defeated anyone. Barack Obama's greatest victory is not that he became the first African American president of the United States of America, but that he successfully united the broken and ever so divided black community.

If Barack Obama was just another hard working white-collared citizen and not the president of the United States of America, would you have embraced him the same? If you saw him walking down the streets in the hood, would you show him some love? The answer is most likely, "No. " You would probably laugh at how he was dressed, criticize the way that he talked and spread rumors about the way that he walked. Nothing about Barack Obama's persona reflects the hood, yet African Americans (rich and poor) supported him. Polls showed that Barack Obama received 96% of the African American vote. This statistic indicates that African Americans are in desperate need of new black leaders and that you do not have to act like a "nigga" in order for people to embrace you in the hood.

Barack Obama is the epitome of a successful black man; the word "strength" in its physical form. He inspires us all! His existence alone encourages the disheartened and cultivates the minds of young people, daring them to dream big. That is the catalyst which will essentially catapult the African American race into a new stratosphere in which our old ceiling will be the floor of a new level of excellence.

There is a strong need for new leaders within the African American community. With all due respect to Al Sharpton, Jesse Jackson and Dorothy Tillman, their time has come and gone. This is a new day and a new age. In today's society the hip hop culture is setting the course of the African American race. Rappers have replaced activists. There are no more great orators, just lyricists with a lot to prove and little to say. We need young leaders that were born in the hip hop era who understand the mindset of the younger generation to carry the torch.

Where are our young, black, socially conscious leaders today? You don't become Martin Luther King overnight. It is a process that begins at an early age. From high school, you start to build your resume (e.g., class president, team captain, editor for the school paper) and develop leadership skills that will prepare you for the road ahead. All the senior level black activists (i.e., those who were a part of the Civil Rights Movement) have reached the age of retirement. There is a group of middle level black activists (Tavis Smiley, Michael Eric Dyson, Cornel West, etc.) who are prepared to step in and fill their shoes; but it appears, at least on the surface, there are few first-level activists in-training prepared to fill the void that the middle level activists will leave.

Young people seem too concerned with being "fancy" (Hair done... nails done...everything did), gettin' their swag on, or goin' to the club and gettin' white boy wasted. In a land of followers, this world desperately needs leaders; people who are not afraid to go against the grain. Those who refuse to toe the line or follow the status quo just to be better received or more well-known. You have to be willing to be unpopular and alienated from your peers for the greater good of a higher mission. According to rapper Wiz Khalifa, it's quite normal for young people to waste time getting drunk and smoking weed. It's just "living young and wild and free."

Being sloppy drunk and high out of your mind serves no purpose other than to provide a temporary escape, but when you sober up or come down from your high all the issues you and the African American race are facing will still be there. There needs to be a deeper awareness for the events happening around us that are impacting the black community and less focus on the trivial topics that possess intrinsic value within gossip circles, but have no bearing on the overall direction of the African American race. Our focus has to shift towards critical thinking. We have to tune our collective consciousness and start back developing young leaders. Will the young black activists please STAND UP!

6

HIP HOPOCRISY

"My business is about the streets, but my business ain't in the streets."
—Puff Daddy (*Notorious* the movie)

It's not just about looking back at slavery and pointing out all the social inequities that have led to the problems black people face today. It's also beneficial to look at today's society and identify the hindrances that are impeding the progress and preventing blacks, as a whole, from prospering. Atop the list is the hip hop movement. What started as just another genre of music has blossomed into something much greater. Hip hop is more than just music, it's a language…it's a style…it's an attitude…it's an image…it's a culture!

The hip hop culture has played as big a role as any other vehicle in driving a wedge between the state of mind of African Americans back during the Civil Rights Movement and the mentality of many young black people today. It's painfully obvious to me that we are currently in a recession with regards to young black leaders (activists). Even worse is that it appears we are apathetically engaged in social politics and married to all things hip hop. Most would rather *Watch the Throne* than watch a documentary on The Black Wall Street—that sh*t Kray!

Before the hip hop culture was formed, the African American culture existed. Long after the last rapper has spit his last bar, the African American culture will still be in existence. The question is, "When we finally survey the damage, how many years will we (African

Americans) have squandered focusing our attention in the wrong direction—materialism, consumerism, swaggerism—and at what cost?"

The monetary success of the hip hop industry is undeniable. The industry has grossed billions of dollars in revenue year after year and given us successful black entrepreneurs and industry moguls. But in the process, the music has become exceedingly more explicit, more misogynistic and less thought provoking. A music that was once meant to give voice to the political struggles and racial inequalities of African Americans has now become a nuisance to its own race.

At some point it became more about making money than making a statement. Major record labels began signing rap artists to lucrative record deals and with that hip hop went from being an underground genre of music to the top of the Billboard charts.

Today, the hip hop culture stretches far beyond the urban black community into the heart of mainstream media. Major corporations are using rap, or some form of hip hop in their TV advertisements. Even President Obama solicited help from rappers to promote his 2008 presidential campaign. Investors are partnering with rappers to purchase sports franchises. TV producers are targeting rappers for raunchy new reality shows that portray black women in a negative light (e.g., *Love & Hip Hop*) and the list goes on and on.

Thanks to the successful integration of hip hop into mainstream media, an impoverished state of mind is now a nationwide phenomenon. Anyone, regardless of their socioeconomic status, that buys into the backwards thinking, negative imagery, and narcissistic beliefs expressed in rap songs are suffering from an impoverished state of mind. Why? Because rap music is about urban street life, so whoever embraces the thought process, voluntarily embraces an impoverished state of mind. Even young black business professionals find themselves getting caught up in the hype. Successful black men with six-figure salaries wanting to feel empowered or "bossy" are buying out the bar and "making it rain" in the club, doing their best Lil' Wayne impersonation. Even U.S. Olympic swimmer Ryan Lochte had a custom diamond-encrusted grill in the form of the American flag made for him to sport around London in the 2012 Olympics.

It seems like the whole country has bought into the façade of the hip hop culture; or at least on the surface. In reality, it's only the younger hip hop generation. Rap music, by in large, is still viewed negatively in today's society. The hip hop culture is accepted by the mass culture to the degree in which it can be exploited to make money. Beyond that point, it's popularity and appeal is limited to those within the culture. If you don't believe me, guys, try wearing earrings or a gold grill to a job interview. Walk in and greet your potential new employer by saying, "What it do?" I don't know what it do, but I can tell you what it won't do is get you hired. A better word to describe the relationship between the hip hop culture and today's society is "tolerated."

How Hip Hop is *Screwing* the African American Community

One day during my freshman year in college, I walked into my teammate Roger's room while he was playing music. I had heard all styles of rap from hard core gangster to socially conscious, but the sound I heard escaping his room was foreign to my ears.

"What is that?" I asked.

"H-town baby! That's what we do…we chop and screw!" he laughed and replied.

Chopping and screwing refers to a method of remixing rap music by slowing down the tempo and applying certain effects—skipping beats and record scratching—to create a "chopped and screwed" rendition of the original song. This form of remixing was made famous by a local Houston disc jockey, DJ Screw, in the early 1990s. It is believed by Screw enthusiasts that every song sounds better chopped and screwed. Roger was no different.

Over the next four years of college, Roger tortured me with his

DJ Screw mix tapes. I would have rather listened to country music (my least favorite genre) than chopped and screwed rap. I couldn't understand why anyone would willingly listen to this style of music. By slowing the tempo down, it made every rapper sound like an intoxicated Rick Ross. After a few years of college, one would think that the sound would have grown on me, but when I graduated I felt the same way about chopping and screwing as I did the first time we crossed paths in Roger's dorm room.

Screwing or this deliberate attempt to slowdown a pace is not limited to the Houston rap scene. It's being employed by the entire hip hop industry. While the techniques may be vastly different, the goal is ultimately the same—retarded pace. By slowing down our pace (growth), the hip hop industry and its leaders continue their reign in power, as the hip hop culture has arguably set the course of the African American race for the past decade.

In 2007, rapper Jay-Z released a song entitled, "30 Something." While the overall theme of the song is Jay-Z's supposed maturation, the lyrics contradict his message. Throughout the song he continuously declares "30's the new 20 nigga!" That doesn't sound like a man striving to mature. In fact, it sounds like someone desperately trying to hang on to their youth (The irony of the entire song is that Jay-Z was pushing 40 when he released the track.)

There is an ulterior motive for Jay-Z's shrewd declaration. He's an aging rapper. With most of Jay-Z's original fan base now over the age of thirty, he made a daring attempt to preserve his audience. If he can keep his fan base in their 20-year-old state of mind, he can hopefully keep them as consumers of hip hop—music, fashion, etc. Time waits for nobody. This notion that 30 is the new 20 is ridiculous. If 30 is the new 20, is 20 the new 10? Should everyone in their twenties trade-in their cars and go back to riding bicycles? I'm looking for the fountain of youth just like everyone else, but pretending that you're 10 years younger to justify immature behavior is not the answer. Don't fall for the propaganda! Don't allow the hip hop culture to slow our growth.

Embrace your maturation and all that it entails. As you feel yourself starting to grow out of your youth, don't fight to hold on. Let it go! The best is yet to come.

Black Professional Athletes and Hip Hop

Sports have always been a method of change in our society. The undeniable success of early professional black athletes helped tear down the racial barrier in sports and subsequently American culture. If you look back on the history of African Americans and the impact of professional athletes like Jackie Robinson, Wilma Rudolph, Muhammad Ali, Jim Brown, Jesse Owens, Tommie Smith and John Carlos, you quickly realize just how influential sports figures were in the advancement of the Civil Rights Movement.

Today, black professional athletes serve as great ambassadors of the hip hop movement, helping to further hip hop music's popularity throughout the world. Black professional athletes, once celebrated for helping to progress the black community, are now partnering with a movement that is threatening to unravel the efforts of the Civil Rights Movement and damage the black community beyond repair.

While hip hop music represents only a small percentage of the overall music industry revenue, blacks dominate two of the three major American sports—basketball and football. Over 75% of the NBA is African American (67% of the NFL). Statistics suggest that of that 75%, about a third grew up in poverty; thus, they more than likely identify with the hip hop culture.

Whereas most white men would not listen to hip hop, most cannot survive without watching their sports. Thus, merging hip hop with professional sports has taken the music to new heights. America loves their athletes, so no matter what they do we attempt to embrace them; whether it's steroids in baseball or hip hop in basketball (though I'm certainly not equating the two).

I watch *SportsCenter* regularly and not a show goes by without one of the anchors throwing out some random slang, or making reference to one of the latest rap songs in the middle of a highlight. "Kobe goes up for three…and he is stuntin' like my daddy!" As ridiculous as it may sound, the message is loud and clear. It demonstrates the power and popularity of the hip hop culture. TV producers and directors realize how important it is to be able to connect with this audience. Hip hop is no longer just music for the poor urban kids.

That does not mean, all of a sudden, middle-age white men will become huge Lil' Weezy fans, it just means that now rap music can be played in the stadium during commercial breaks and pre-game warm-ups without causing fans to head for the exits. I refer back to the word "tolerated."

What also makes black athletes such advocates of hip hop (besides them enjoying the music) is that they, similar to rappers, are young with lots of money. They are among the few people in this world who can actually live out the scenes of these fictitious rap videos (or go bankrupt attempting to), whether it's buying dozens of luxury cars or buying out the bar at a club.

Rappers and professional athletes alike live in a fantasy world. It's not reality. You see them with their luxury cars, expensive jewelry and beautiful women walking around with their ball-player swag rockin' their custom diamond wrist watch and chain, representing the hip hop image to the fullest.

Like rappers, athletes are not forced to conform to the standards that everyone else has to working in Corporate America. At the "office," they can rock their hair in any style they choose, or from head to toe be covered in tattoos. They have total autonomy.

Many come to post-game press conferences all "iced out" looking like they just stepped on stage at a rap concert. Then they speak into the microphone and though they may be draped in a quarter-million dollars, their speech is poor—struggling to put sentences together and using slang as a filler to get them from one fragmented sentence to the next…"Naw mean?"

There are times during post-game interviews when I cringe as I listen to some of the young black men speaking. It hurts my heart to see young black men in a position of power who struggle to piece together two sentences and choose to use slang instead of proper English. That decision speaks volumes about their character. It says that they either don't care about their public image, or they enjoy being portrayed as a rich uneducated kid from the hood.

I'm all for freedom of expression, but there's a time and place for everything. In front of the media cameras with millions of young kids who idolize them watching is neither the time nor the place, but I'm convinced that some young black professional athletes just don't know any other way to speak. If so, it's understandable as we've already established that many grew up in the hood where few people use proper English.

However, if these same black athletes have enough money to spend $50,000 on jewelry, surely they can afford to hire a speech coach if proper English was a priority, but it's not. Their struggle to use proper English is not incompetence, it's apathy—lack of interest. That's the effect of the hip hop culture. It encourages slang and broken English. In fact, the use of proper English is viewed as lame.

Lebron James and Dwyane Wade both grew up in the hood and embrace the hip hop culture, yet they are fairly well-spoken. Do they sometimes use the incorrect tense or mispronounce a word or two...of course—that's from years of practicing bad habits in the hood. But you can see the effort being made in every interview. It's because they made a conscious decision to improve their public speaking skills. Maybe they did it because conducting interviews was an area of insecurity and they desired to get better. Maybe they have good PR people who advised them of the financial impact—being well-spoken makes them more marketable. Whatever the reason, I appreciate the effort from two of the NBA's most polarizing stars today. I can't speak directly to Lebron's situation, but I grew up about 4 blocks from Dwyane. I can attest to the type of environment he was raised in. I know for certain it required him to make a conscious effort to improve his speech.

There are other examples like NBA veteran Jalen Rose and current NBA player Baron Davis. Both were raised in the hood, but choose to be articulate speakers. Rose is now a basketball analyst for ESPN. He also recently established the Jalen Rose Leadership Academy—a charter school in his hometown of Detroit. Davis is also well connected to his community. In 2008 his production company (Verso Entertainment) made a documentary on LA gangs. But I suspect that there are some black people who question Rose and Davis' blackness because of their improved speech. We've all been socialized to some degree and have bought into the ideology that slang and broken English is somehow a black thing…far be it.

In contrast to Baron Davis and Jalen Rose, there is former NBA basketball all-star Allen Iverson—someone who personifies hip hop and seemingly suffers from an impoverished state of mind. Allen was raised by his single teenage mother in a rough section of Hampton VA. Through his athletic gift, he was blessed with the opportunity to attend Georgetown University and play in the NBA for over a decade—earning millions of dollars in salary income and endorsements in the process. However, despite all the money and exposure to the world that being a professional athlete provides, Iverson appears determined to remain true to his hood upbringing. At 37 years of age, you can still catch Iverson in his sneakers, oversized pants saggin' off his 165 pound frame, oversized tee shirt swallowing his torso, fitted cap cocked and ice dripping off his tatted up neck and arms. All that is missing is a stage name and a microphone.

What is Hip Hop?

It's easy to look at something you don't fully understand and place a generic label on it. I played football for the majority of my early life and on more than one occasion I've run into people who've labeled the game as barbaric, overlooking all the strategy and mental execution required by the game. On every occasion these were people who admittedly did not fully understand the game. If they did, they would understand that football is a thinking game that is more similar to chess than checkers.

There are people who don't fully understand hip hop, so they label it as shallow and mindless music. I grew up a hip hop fanatic. It might be many adjectives, but mindless is not one. There is a tremendous amount of thought put into the imagery and lyrics, which is a very scary thought. It begs the question, "What are rappers trying to convey in the content of their songs and videos?"

Hip hop has the potential to be a great genre of music, from the beats, to the lyrics and rhyme scheme. It fuses several eras of music together to create its own unique sound. The genre of music itself is fascinating; it's the rappers who give the hip hop industry a black eye. I understand hip hop. I know that there's more to it than sex, money and drugs; but if this represents the majority of hip hop music being put out on the shelves, what more do we, as consumers, have to shape our opinion? There are rappers who are still making good music, but they are few and far between.

Hip hop music is an art form. Thus, those who create the sound are considered artists. However, the term "artist" is extremely misleading—a misnomer even. An artist, in its purest sense, is someone who has a deep affection for their art. He would never jeopardize the integrity of the art. An artist has a strong sense of self. He strives to be unique. It's what separates his work of genius from the masses. 90's rap groups like A Tribe Called Quest and Public Enemy—though vastly different in sound—represented true artistry.

Rap artists today are not interested in creating their own sound. They are interested in what sells. Instead of being in-tune with their creative spirit, they're merely researching what is popular and recreating the sound. That's why most rap songs sound the same. This is the equivalent of the entire art industry painting the same picture only changing the color scheme. While color can significantly influence and change the mood of a painting, how many times can you stare at a variation of the same Mona Lisa painting before you get bored?

Rap Baking

Trying to create a hit rap song is like trying to bake a cake. In order to make a song that everyone will like, you have to include certain key ingredients. Nothing makes the "cake" rise better than a few cups of gangsta, a tablespoon of profanity, two teaspoons of bragging, a stick of money (references), add a pinch of swagger, a catchy punch line and combine. It's actually a pretty easy recipe to follow.
For example:

> *You dudes with attitude is bad news*
> *My nine will sing you're a$$ blues*
> *You know what…I'm in a bad mood*
> *You niggas should back up off me*
> *Hammer tucked softly*
> *I got shots to give any nigga tryna defrost me!*

Let's break it down…gangsta…check! Money references…check! Profanity…check! Punch line…check! Overall swag…check! If the taste is not to your liking, you can play around with the recipe. If you want to make it a little less sweet, throw in a little misogyny; or if you want it to be more tart, zest in some more profanity.

Paranoia in Hip Hop

There is a lack of interaction between black men and black women today. There are a number of issues that have lead to this problem, but hip hop helps fuel the fire. Rap lyrics encourage this behavior and add to the pre-existing paranoia. Lyrics like, "You think he's your man, but you really just gettin' ran thru." With the hip hop industry being predominately black male, black women struggle to make it in the industry. The few black women who succeed—Lil' Kim being the most infamous—understand how to successfully balance the power. Since most rap songs paint women as sex objects, they use this dynamic to their advantage.

You wanna see some a$$
I wanna see some cash
Keep dem dollas comin'
And dat's gone make me dance
Make it rain trick
Make it...make it rain trick!

Instead of being the prey, female rappers use their bodies as power and reverse the roles. They become predators and men become preys (tricks). Due to this, the relationship between young black men and women has been reduced to transactional—women looking for men with the fattest pockets and men looking for women with the fattest... you get the picture.

Rap lyrics paint the picture of being a predator or prey. Black men can either choose to prey on black women, or have black women prey on them and vice versa. Everyone's so afraid of being played that they put up a wall. Black men treat black women like they're a dime-a-dozen and black women act nonchalant about black men—neither side willing to allow themselves to look vulnerable. As a result, statistics show that 42% of African American women are unmarried.

This statistic is a result of what I refer to as the "Street Merchant Paradox." A few years back, my wife and I went on a cruise to celebrate our anniversary. It was a week-long tour of several islands along the Western Caribbean. About the fifth day, everyone was called down to the auditorium for a mandatory safety briefing. Our next scheduled stop was Ocho Rios, Jamaica. The crew wanted to make sure everyone—who planned to leave the ship—understood the rules of engagement when interacting with the locals.

"Don't talk to anyone unless you're interested in buying something!" one crew member said. Then, he went further to say, "If possible, try to avoid eye contact all together."

"Is it really that serious?" I thought to myself.

It wasn't until the ship docked and we walked down the ramp into a sea of street merchants that I fully understood the gravity of the situation. I found myself relying on my training as we attempted to work our way through the makeshift marketplace at the foot of the dock. It's hard to ignore people when they are coming at you from every direction. But with a stiff neck and eyes fixed on the horizon, I clinched my wife's hand and we made our way to the other side.

This passive-aggressive strategy of eluding people is not limited to the Jamaican marketplace. Here in America, black women have mastered the art. They use it quite successfully in avoiding potential husbands. If statistics show that 42% of black women are unwed, why would they deliberately avoid interacting with their male counterpart?

On the surface, black women's behavior appears rude and standoffish; but their actions are not without merit. Contrary to popular belief, we don't live in a society full of bitter and angry black women. This anti-social behavior is simply a defense mechanism. From the point they leave the house until they return home, black women are bombarded by black men approaching them from every direction. As a result, black men's uniqueness has been watered down. We are merely viewed as a bunch of street merchants unidentifiable amongst the masses? We might have a different pitch, but we're all selling the same thing. Thus, there is no motivation for black women to want to entertain a conversation. If you think this buyer and seller relationship is not influenced by the hip hop culture...think again.

False Sense of Blackness: "I'm so hood!"

Back home in the hood all black people looked alike, walked alike and talked alike, but when I got to college that dynamic changed. On campus we shared the same skin tone, but that was about all we had in common. As I mentioned before, I viewed these blacks as sellouts or "wannabes." In my mind being black meant greeting me by saying, "What's good" or rockin' Sean John and a fitted (cap). I had a false sense of blackness and I fought hard to retain it. At no point did I consciously say to myself, "stay black," but in retrospect I can remember growing my hair out, increasing my slang and doing everything in my power not to resemble the black people I was surrounded by on campus. It was my way of staying true to my culture.

For those of you who might be thinking along the same lines, I say emphatically, "Don't mistake black poverty for black pride." Rappers use phrases like "I'm from the gutta" or "I'm so hood" as if it makes us who we are. Being "gutta" or from the "hood" has absolutely nothing to do with being black. It makes reference to your social economic status. Unfortunately African Americans have been associated with poverty for so long that it's hard to distinguish the two.

Being black is synonymous with being poor and being poor (or from the hood) is synonymous with hip hop. In algebra when trying to solve an equality, the transitive property states, if $a = b$ and $b = c$, then $a = c$. This helps explain the connection between blacks and hip hop. Being black = being poor and being poor (or hood) = hip hop, thus being black = hip hop.

I've been asked on occasion, "why do you hate hip hop?" I don't hate hip hop. I'm opposed to its principles and what it stands for. It's nothing personal. I'm opposed to any industry that poses a threat to the growth of the African American community. I cannot support an industry where you gain credibility by negativity. You're a nobody in the rap game unless you sell yourself as an ex-con, ex-killer, ex-dopeboy turned rapper.

I do however hate what the word "hood" has become. It's too commercialized. I could have titled this book "Hood State-of-Mind," but then it would have sounded too much like the title of a rap song and taken on a celebratory effect. The reality is "the hood" is just a euphemism for "poverty," so let's stop celebrating it and call it what it is…you're poor! When did we, as African Americans, begin celebrating mediocrity? At what point did being poor become cool? It's a direct reflection of the hip hop culture which celebrates the hood like it's an accomplishment or an achievement.

Every time the word "hood" is referenced in a rap song, it's usually followed by some silly stereotype. I'm from the hood…"I let my pants hang low" or in the hood…"we ride Chevy's on chrome." Growing up in the hood taught me many lessons, but what I took from my experience had little to do with "letting my pants hang low" or "riding Chevys on chrome." You (the individual) can choose to embrace whatever aspects you want. I believe life and death are in the power of the tongue. Rappers choose to speak words of death. They embrace what I refer to as the super-negative aspects of the hood. Super-negative simply means they focus on all the superficial and negative topics possible. The content of every rap song I hear revolves around the same topics. Either all the fancy cars, big chains, big rims and fresh clothes they have, or all the women they have, drugs they've sold and people they've shot.

On the other hand, I'm from the hood, but I choose to embrace what I refer to as the deeper-positive aspects of the hood; such as drive, determination and the ability to overcome adversity. If you were born into poverty the odds are you will remain there, so anyone who can find the strength to rise above the strongholds of poverty is an incredibly resilient individual. The perseverance that individual develops in the process will last a lifetime.

If rappers are so intrigued by hood life, why are they striving so hard to sell records and make it out? Don't believe all the crap these rappers are selling. It's all propaganda. Rappers are worse than politicians when it comes to saying one thing and doing another. One minute they're "in the kitchen with soda…tryna stretch out the coca" the next minute they're venture capitalists investing in professional basketball teams. Which one is it? Are you a dope boy or a private investor? I for one am tired of the hypocrisy in the hip hop industry.

I finally had the chance to sit down and watch the movie *Notorious*—a story portraying the life and death of The Notorious B.I.G. The movie was unremarkable, but there was one part in the movie that stood out. It was a line from actor Derek Luke who was playing the role of Sean "Puffy" Combs. In response to Biggie selling drugs and hanging in the street, Puff stated, "My business is about the streets, but my business ain't in the streets."

So it's alright to talk about all the hustlin' and killin' just as long as it remains that…just talk. What about all the people that hang onto every word and believe all the nonsense these rapper's are spittin'? What about the destruction to the black community that's being caused by these words? These words of death are destroying as many young black minds as crack cocaine. And rappers have the same "As long as my family is eating" mentality as drug dealers. They don't care about how many families and communities they poison in the process.

The problem is that if you were once a drug dealer and are now a rapper, you've turned your life around. You went from making crumbs doing something that was illegal, to making millions doing something that's legal. I applaud them for finding their creative niche and turning it into a prosperous career, but they've allowed their gift to become perverted somewhere along the way.

These major record labels take advantage of hungry young rappers. I understand that when you're a poor young teenager and you have major record labels throwing money at you, it's hard to resist. If they tell you to rap a nursery rhyme you would do it; because you know there are a thousand other young black men on the outside looking in, dying to be where you are. Once you make the decision to go down that path, whether you agree with everything that's going on or not, all you can do is defend your decision and keep moving forward. What's good for hip hop is good for everyone in the industry; so it's in everyone's best interest to grow the market. But at some point it has to be about more than just money.

I've worked in the corporate world and at the end of the day all that matters is how much money is being added to the company's bottom line. Record companies are no different. Behind every rapper there is a greedy corporate executive with his hand out. Even the rappers who are independent of a major record label face the pressures of producing hits. If you can't sell you won't make it in the industry. Most feel they have to maintain a certain street image to appeal to their audience.

Let's again use Jay-Z for example—since he seems to be widely regarded as the people's champion. With him, everything's a drug related innuendo. Try listening to five random Jay-Z songs and see if you can make it through the tracks without him mentioning: the kitchen, pots, baking soda or boiling water. I guess he's familiar with rap baking.

Jay-Z obviously can't still portray the role of street life anymore, so he makes every attempt to draw parallels from the dope game to the rap game in his music. That's the only way he feels he can remain relevant with the emergence of fresh young talent every day. It's an exaggerated attempt to stay connected to his audience. As a rapper you must personify the hood, so everyone in the hood (or infatuated with it) will identify with you. In the hood, people refer to these rappers as if they are their best friend, "Jay did this…Weezy said that." In reality, they are more like your worst enemy. No real friend would lie and deceive you the way rappers attempt to. The struggles you face on a day-to-day, they only rap about. They play dress up in the streets then retreat to their suburban oasis with their personal chef and maids; yet they are so hood! The hypocrisy in hip hop is absolutely absurd.

Rappers go between fantasy and reality from one bar to the next and some listeners struggle to differentiate. It would be different if we were talking about another profession. Take comedians for example, they make up stories all the time, but their audience understands that the goal is to make them laugh, by any means necessary. Unless most of these rappers have already stood trial in a murder case and were found not guilty, thus unable to be retried (based on double jeopardy laws), why would they publicly confess to murder?

If I were a cold case detective, instead of wasting hours shuffling through old files, I would just listen to rap music. With all the people rappers are claiming they've shot and killed, it should be easy to find evidence.

New rappers' number one goal is to establish street credibility, so they talk about how much drugs they've sold, or how many times they've been shot. Once that's established, rappers need to appeal to their target market, so they rap about materials (cars, clothes, jewelry, etc.) they believe are desirable to their audience. But, the key is, it has to be things that are desirable yet grossly unattainable. They use these persuasive images to paint a picture for you and make you idolize and envy them—wishing you were in their shoes.

They make you believe that having money is all about poppin' tags, poppin' bottles, and poppin' off a different woman every day of the week. Since most rappers are men, ladies you take the backseat role. Your only goal in life is to be with the biggest baller and stand by their side while they pop tags and pop bottles; as displayed by the video vixens in every rap video.

It's all an image. The irony in hip hop is that new artists come on to the scene every year. If you know anything about the industry, you understand that the majority of the revenue from records sales is going directly to the label. After discounting the distributor, marketing and advertising expenses and recording costs, the artist is lucky to see ten cents on every dollar; yet in the videos we see them driving around Bentleys on 30s, wearing one-hundred thousand dollars worth of jewelry and makin' it rain.

It's just a façade. The reality is that most of what you see is rented; it's all props to help sell their image. Labels spend big money to help market their product.

So let me get this straight…rappers come in the game with no money. They brag about all the cars, clothes and jewelry they have and get you to buy into their image. Then, they sell a million records and thanks to you, they are now able to buy all the things that they could only rap about before? Interesting...

Infatuation with Hip Hop

I must admit, it's remarkable how the hip hop industry was able to integrate lower-class black culture into the mainstream media and make it relevant. This caused a fundamental shift in beliefs. Instead of lower-class blacks feeling like they have to conform to the world, the hip hop culture brought the rest of the world to the hood. It's made lower-class blacks feel comfortable with being themselves. Only if the hip hop industry would have focused on the positive aspects of urban black culture rather than glorify the negative, we would have witnessed a revolution of unprecedented proportions. It would have been reminiscent of the 1960s and the Black Power Movement when chants of "Black is beautiful!" rang out in black communities all across the nation.

Today, being from the hood is in vogue; everybody's a gangsta, thug, pimp, player, or dope boy. The hip hop culture has sensationalized and romanticized the hood so much that the hood has become a notable agent in pop culture. As if we don't have enough people living in poverty, now we have actors pretending to be from the hood. Why is the hood so appealing to the broader American culture? That's the real question and problem.

The hood has become so commercialized that you now have young suburban girls slumming through the inner-city looking for their own thug. But they don't want a real thug; they want someone who's a little rough around the edges that can walk-the-walk and talk-the-talk. A real thug however comes with real issues. The suburban ladies want the romanticized image and legendary swagger without all the baggage.

Much of rap's mainstream appeal comes from its beats rather than its lyrics. A great beat and catchy chorus make a song successful. White people listen to rap songs they don't know the words to all the time; as long as they like the beat they will improvise the lyrics.

Above and beyond the beat and chorus, the broader American culture's infatuation with rap is due to the cocky, brass, flamboyant nature of the music. If you are a shy person, it helps you take on the persona of someone who is full of confidence. If you're already confident, it turns you obnoxiously arrogant.

People say you can tell when someone has been using steroids because they become more aggressive and confrontational due to the boost in testosterone. It's commonly referred to as "roid rage." Well the same holds true for the guys who are juiced up on a dose of 50 cent or Weezy. Their lyrics make even the timid feel strong, cocky and ready to take on the world. I call it, "rap rage." Due to this phenomenon, without any data to support my claim, I declare that rap music has been involved in most drive-by shootings in the black community—the shooters certainly weren't listening to Fred Hammond.

The infatuation with hip hop represents everything that is wrong with society today. There is a party spirit that surrounds the hip hop culture and subsequently the mass culture. In every rap video there is usually a club or party scene with the rap artist surrounded by his crew and an entourage of beautiful women. Around every major city on any given Friday or Saturday night there are thousands of people trying to live out their own rap video; men pulling up in Mercedes', Lexus' and Bentleys, picking ladies out the crowd to join them in the VIP; women dressed to impress with their finest weave and make-up standing at the front door of the club expecting VIP treatment. These are not women of the night, or gold diggers looking for a rich athlete to take care of them. These are professional women with multiple degrees and six-figure salaries subjecting themselves to such unbecoming behavior. Why? Because it's not about money, it's about perceived status and wanting to feel important according to an artificial and dangerous construct.

You have to force yourself out of the negative mind state the hip hop culture encourages. One way to remove this counterproductive train of thought from your psyche is to stop quoting lines from rap songs. I know you do it because I was that kid once. There wasn't a line that Jay-Z spit that I didn't spit twice.

"Nigga please! Like short sleeves, I bare (bear) arms!" or my favorite "That's high school making me chase you 'round for months. Have an affair! Act like an adult for once!"

Guys, no more one liners from Jay and Weezy. Ladies, stop buying into everything Beyoncé or Nicki Minaj is saying in their songs. "We like dem boys up top from the BK…know how to flip that money three ways" or "A diva is a female version of a hustla"…really B? I think the Devastating Divas of Delta Sigma Theta might disagree with that definition. Whether you're saying it to be cute or just singing along with the song…stop!

When I was young I can remember sitting around in my room memorizing rap songs. I would rewind the track 20 to 30 times until I knew the exact words and the right flow (pauses and breaks) of the song. Around that time Eightball and MJG were a popular rap duo. One of my favorite songs was entitled, "Pimps." It had a smooth beat and the hook was a sample from an old rhythm and blues song, giving it a real soulful sound. But the lyrics were very vulgar and explicit. Picture me at twelve years old sitting around my room reciting these words:

Part two
It's all the same G
tryin' to school fools, on this P-I-M-P
Lesson one
first you should pull a b*&#h, f%*k her good
next time tell her no, the next time take her dough
oh, you better watch your back too mane
'cause there's a lot of b*&#hes in the world wit much game
Lesson two

watch dat h@e,
don't trust her wit none of yo dough
never let a b*&#h know, how you make yo cash flow
Lesson three
if you don't tell dat h@e who is boss
b*&#hes like to run sh^t
but end up gettin' smacked in the mouth
see a real nigga believe in beatin' dem h@es down
push her head into the wall til you hear dat crackin' sound

No wonder I had an issue respecting women. At the tender age of twelve I was pumping disrespectful, misogynistic lyrics like this into my brain. That coupled with everything I learned about the game in the streets taught me it was either eat or be eaten.

This song basically says, if you're not beating your woman, you're not a real man. If you don't use her for sex and exploit her for money, what is the point of the relationship? If you start having feelings for her and display any act of kindness or affection, you are weak and there are women out there who know the game that will prey on you.

Me listening to "Pimps" back in the 90s is no different from you listening to Lil' Wayne today saying,

I swear you can't f*@k wit me
But I can f*@K yo' girl and make her nut for me
Then slut for me, then kill for me, then steal for me
And of course it'll be yo' cash
Then I'll murder that b*t@h and send her body back to yo' a$$!

It's this type of negative ideology expressed in rap songs that perpetuates domestic violence and keeps young black men and women at odds with each other.

Social Irresponsibility

Just as we all have rights as citizens of the United States of America, I believe we also have a responsibility to preserve the integrity of our society and protect it against nuisances that are detrimental to it.

The negativity expressed in rap music is a larger concern for our society than anyone in the hip hop industry is willing to acknowledge. Why do rappers degrade women and promote violence in their music? The question has been raised time and time again, yet the answer remains in secrecy. Rappers are often asked, but they backpedal away from these types of questions faster than Deon Sanders in the late 80s/early 90s, or the rappers provide a contrived response filled with contradictions.

No matter which rapper is questioned about their lyrics the typical response is, "I'm just taking about my experiences." As a writer I understand that concept. I draw inspiration from many different experiences in my life, both positive and negative, and use them as motivation. Using a negative experience as motivation is one thing, but glorifying it is something entirely different: "Sold dope, sold crack, bought Bentleys, bought em back, nigga can you try that?"

Instead of writing a book aimed at helping impoverished youth escape the hood, I could have chosen to use my street smarts to write something less original and more stereotypical like, *How to Flip a Key in a Week*, or for the ladies, *Get the Doe Without Giving Up the Draws*. It may have become a *New York Times'* best seller, but how would the success of my book promote the general welfare of our society?

I'm not trying to turn you against rap or the hip hop culture as a whole; I'm trying to get you to look at it more objectively. Realize that there is more to rap than just repeating words and bobbing your head to a beat. If you're trying to remember something, what do you do? You write it down over and over, or you continue to repeat it like a chant until you've committed it to memory. The same thing is true of rap lyrics that are constantly repeated. You internalize them and they become a part of you and your thought process. It's been at least ten years since I've heard "Pimps"; however, I could have reproduced the lyrics to the song by memory without looking them up.

I grew up listening to rap. Every morning I would pop in a CD to get ready for school. I carried my headphones around listening to music throughout the day, and usually before I went to bed, I would put in another CD as background noise to help me fall asleep.

When I finally made the decision to stop listening to rap, nothing changed about my love for the music. I was at a stage in my life where I could truly see the negative impact of hip hop on the urban black community. I wanted to affect change in our society, so I told myself, "You have to stop straddling the fence. You're either helping the cause or hurting the cause. There is no in between." On that day, I chose to stop listening to rap.

After being away from rap for some time, I started having withdrawl, so I picked up one of my favorite Mobb Deep albums—*Murda Muzik*—and popped it in the CD player. Within two minutes of listening, I turned it off. Before, I would listen and bob my head to the beat; but after taking a break from rap then coming back, I found myself shaking my head rather than bobbing it. I was listening with a new set of ears, ones that were more sensitive to the words spoken.

7

THE MIGRATION

Migrate: to go from one country, region, [state] or place to another

When I first shared with people my idea of writing a self-empowering book for teenagers and young adults living in the hood, they laughed. When I shared with them some of the book's projected content, they laughed even harder. "You're trying to reach a group of people using a medium that is foreign to them. Young blacks don't read," they said. "Your proposed topics are too sophisticated for your target audience." They felt that if I was lucky enough to get some of you to open the book, the content should be similar to that of a Dr. Seuss book—since most people in the hood are uneducated. I'm glad I didn't listen to the naysayers and that you proved them wrong. Who's laughing now?

I could have allowed the pessimism to influence my approach. Understanding that the majority of my audience would probably prefer to listen to music than read a book, I could have written My Story in bars like a rap song:

> *Growin' up against the grain,*
> *Victim of circumstance, no father, so my mother took the blame*
> *As she tried to maintain a steady 9 to 5*
> *Pops was somewhere in the streets gettin' high as the sky*
> *Blood shot eyes, no worries, no doubts*
> *So without a father figure in my sight*
> *I grew addicted to the street life*

And when times got hard I would starve
So thru my hunger my hustle grew
Next thing I knew I was on the block blowin' a dice or two...

In all seriousness, throughout this book I've strived to connect with you. But if the entire goal was to help you elevate your mind to a higher level, what benefit would it have been to you if I kept you in your comfort zone? I assumed that everyone who opened this book was ready for a challenge.

Now that you have read this entire book, go back and review the chapters and sections that are most pertinent to you. Look to see if you skimmed over any critical information, or possibly misinterpreted something I said. As I stated before, this book was not meant to tailor fit one specific person; it discusses a generalized collection of issues faced by black people living in urban poverty. Ideally, reading this book helped you gain some valuable knowledge that gave you a better understand of yourself and the broader world around you.

While my focus has been on the urban black community, these issues are not limited to the hood. Some of these issues are nationwide and crossover all race and social classes. However, these issues are more prevalent and damaging to the urban black community.

It was never my intention to tackle every issue in parade detail. My objective was to shine some light on some of the general issues facing the impoverished black community and get you to start thinking critically about them. I could have continued on for at least another 300 pages—expanding the topics and diving deeper into every subject. But rather than attempt to discuss every problem facing the urban black community, I'll ask you to step up and fill in the voids I've left unaddressed.

Think about the issues you are facing directly and attempt to find a solution. Continue to thirst for knowledge. Be critical of information presented to you. Take nothing for granted. Don't allow society to force feed you your thoughts. Define yourself for yourself! Look in the mirror and ask, "Am I happy with what I see?" If the answer is "No" do something about it. Think back, as far as you can remember, over all your life experiences, and try to determine how you became who you are today. Embrace the positive aspects that have helped you move forward and free yourself from the captivity of bad habits.

I hope this book has served as an interstate highway to connect you from an impoverished state to an empowered state. As you move from one state to the next, I can guarantee you there will be a traffic jam or two—people impeding your progress and slowing you down. There are people who will put you in a box or judge you by the person you were rather than the person you have become. As you work on bettering yourself don't let the negativity of outsiders make you revert back to who you were. The fact of the matter is that people change and unfortunately it's not always for the better. I've watched as people I used to envy (because of their stand-up qualities) have lost character and standards, while I've witnessed others with troubled backgrounds turn their lives around. So allow all the finger pointers and naysayers to say what they want. Don't allow any of their negativity to penetrate your mind. Just focus on improving.

Sometimes we quit too soon, right when we're on the brink of a breakthrough. The road is rough, but such is life. I've done some crazy and stupid things, much of which I'm not proud of, but I've learned to take the bitter with the sweet. Regardless of how successful I become, I now realize that the greatest gift is in the pursuit and I will always appreciate the road I traveled to get here.

As you change, your situation may not. As a matter of fact it might get worse, but keep fighting! If life knocks you down…keep fighting! If you fall short of your dream…keep fighting! If you don't get accepted to your preferred college…keep fighting! If you don't earn a scholarship…keep fighting! If you can't find work…keep fighting! If you lose a loved one…keep fighting! If you become ill…keep fighting! No matter what life hands you…KEEP FIGHTING!

As you unmask some of the layers, it's also likely that you will go through an identity crisis. You will see a change occurring in you and you won't recognize the person in the mirror. You will feel the urge to revert back to the old you. But in the midst of the crisis you must keep fighting!

Even now, after I've completed the necessary steps and reconditioned my mind, I still struggle with certain aspects of my personality that have changed. Ten years ago, I would have made a mockery of the man I see in the mirror today. Sometimes I revert back to that childhood mindset and I facetiously say to myself, "You a lame!" The thought is usually triggered by me engaging in some activity that I never would have done back in the hood like listening to some jazz music, going to the opera, shaving my facial hair, or the fact that I choose not to curse. Everything about me had to mature in order for me to become the man I am today. This maturation has brought about much positive change. Rather than fight the change, I decided to embrace it. I now refer to myself as a "self-proclaimed lame."

As much as I would like to believe that you can spend a few days reading this book, go to bed and wake up a brand new person, that is not reality; but you can wake up with a new mindset and approach to life. Reading a book cannot erase years of practicing bad habits. There are some habits you can change in the immediate, but realistically it will probably take just as long as it did to create those bad habits, to fully get rid of them. Habits (good or bad) are not easily broken. It requires a tremendous amount of effort and a wholehearted commitment to change. It has to be a total commitment, because there will be setbacks along the way and if you are unsure of your decision, you will quit prematurely.

There will be people who will read this book who are motivated to change. They will start making steps in the right direction, but as the days and weeks pass by, they will resort back to their old way of doing things; not because they have given up, but because old habits are hard to change.

Take something as simple as putting a roll of toilet tissue on the holder. Growing up, my family always put the roll on the holder with the tissue dispensing from underneath the roll. My wife grew up putting the roll on the holder with the tissue dispensing over the top of the roll. When we got married and moved in together, this presented a huge problem! I resisted the change, but eventually gave in and we decided to use her over-the-top tissue loading method (I bet you never knew loading toilet tissue was so scientific). It's been almost five years since we tied the knot and converted to the OTT tissue method, but if you were to come to our home today, you might find one or two rolls still being dispensed from underneath (those darn old habits).

Contrary to popular belief, people do not dictate their actions, patterns do. Each day is made up of a series of patterns—from the way you get out of bed to the way you prepare to go to sleep. Some people's lives are more regimented than others, but even the most spontaneous people have patterns that govern their day. Habits are nothing more than an event that is repeated several times until a pattern is developed. If you get in the habit of doing the right thing, it will become natural to you.

Once you rise above poverty, rather than being praised for your perseverance, in a counterintuitive way, you might be viewed as the black sheep of the family because you made it out. Feeling like you've abandoned the family or turned your nose up at them, the rest of the family might reject you. Just remember to reach back and take others with you. That doesn't mean become the family's personal bank—though helping a family member might require a financial investment. Helping might require investing your time and driving a family member to and from work, until they are able to obtain reliable transportation. It might require sharing knowledge about finding financial aid with a family member looking to go back to school. Sometimes we get consumed by our own lives and struggle to realize that there are others around us hurting who could use a helping hand.

Sometimes success will also make us lose sight of the larger picture. Don't lose focus on the goal—social and racial equality. Don't measure your success by the standards of society. I'm not sure when blacks' success morphed into exclusivity—velvet roped VIP sections, unlimited top-shelf bottles of Champagne, A-list crowds—but Blacks' success, in its archaic form, used to be measured by your accomplishments relative to its impact on black culture. It wasn't about exclusivity. It was about cultural progress and solidarity. If you read about some of the successful African Americans in our history (W.E.B. Du Bois, Langston Hughes, Thurgood Marshall, Mary McLeod Bethune), they all had one thing in common. Their contributions helped advance the African American race in some fashion. There is nothing wrong with pursuing personal wealth, but understand that there has to be a greater purpose for this wealth other than to flaunt it. What will be your contribution to the growth and success of the African American race?

You have read and armed yourself with the necessary information, now you are prepared to take your journey out of impoverishment. It's not necessarily about moving to a better zip code. It's about freeing your mind from the bondage that is an impoverished community. There will be bumps along the road, but take comfort in knowing you have the strength for the fight. As the old adage goes, "knowledge is power" and by virtue of reading this book you have empowered yourself and generations to come. May your off-spring enjoy the path that you have paved. Thank you for staying the course. Be blessed and enjoy life's riches!

ACKNOWLEDGEMENTS

Never have I been more sincere when I say that I must first thank my Lord and Savior, Jesus Christ. This book was inspired by a collection of people and events throughout my early life—both positive and negative. Thanks to Him, all things ultimately worked together for my good and provided me with a testimony to help motivate and inspire others.

This project spanned over five years and several milestones including marriage and childbirth. That said, it would have been impossible to devote time to writing this book—while working a full-time job—without the steadfast support and encouragement of my amazing wife, Leanne. Being a wife, mother and business partner can sometimes be a thankless job, but I would be remiss if I didn't express my deepest gratitude for your patience, understanding and adept editorial assistance throughout this exciting yet incredibly stressful project. With you by my side, no mountain seems insurmountable or dream unattainable.

I finished the first full rough draft of this manuscript almost two years ago. After the birth of my daughter, I sat on it for a year in search of an editor. I interviewed several editors who struggled to grasp the concept of the book—to say the least. Just as I was beginning to feel discouraged by my lack of progress, in what appeared as coincidence but I know was God's perfect plan, I was introduced to my editor, Dave Krump, by a mutual friend. From our first conversation you understood and enthusiastically embraced this project. Your thought-provoking feedback and suggestions were invaluable. You challenged me and you never backed down from a fight. Sometimes you won the battle, other times I was victorious. The results of our debates are evident in this great book that we both can be proud of. Simply stated, thank you!

A special thank you to the two young models, Antonio Watkins and my goddaughter Taylor Jones (as well as their parents), for helping me execute the vision for the cover. You both were amazing! I also want to thank Denise Billups, Matt Duckett, Cyrus Dowlatshahi and Laura Shelley for their assistance with the project.

Much credit is deserved to my mother, Pearlie. Since the days of Pee Wee football your love and support has been unwavering. No matter what I've pursued—college degree, professional football career, professional writing career—you've always been there. Words cannot express how significant your presence has been in my life.

I'm also very thankful to the rest of my family, my brother, Demarius, sister, Taanika, father, Sherman and late grandmother, Willie B. In order to share my story, I had to share our story. Your willingness and sacrifice helped make this book come alive for its readers with real life stories.

Last but not least, I want to acknowledge my beautiful daughter, Zoe. Daddy loves you! You are my heart. Even before you stepped foot on this earth, you provided much inspiration. Shortly after the halfway point of writing this book, your mother and I learned that we were going to be parents. Just the thought of bringing you into this world provided me with the motivation I needed to stay the course. Twelve to fifteen years from now when you're reading this book, the one thing I want you to take away from it is that your Dad tried to make a difference in the world. I trust that you will do the same.

CPSIA information can be obtained at www.ICGtesting.com
Printed in the USA
LVOW100324250113

317177LV00013B/240/P

REFERENCES

Alridge, D. B. (2005). Introduction: Hip hop in history: past, present, and future. Journal of African American History, 90(3), 190.

Baugh, J. (2000). Beyond Ebonics: Linguistic pride and racial prejudice. New York: Oxford University Press.

Caramanica, J. (2010). Seeping out of Houston, slowly. New York Times, 26.

Chepesiuk, R. (2007). Black gangsters of Chicago. Fort Lee: Barricade Books

Clark, R. P. (2010). The glamour of grammar: A guide to the magic and mystery of practical English. New York: Little, Brown and Company, a division of Hachett Book Group, Inc.

Coley, R.J. (2011). A strong start: Positioning young black boys for educational success. Educational Testing Services, 1-5.

Combs, S. (Producer), & Tillman Jr., G. (Director). (2009). Notorious [Motion Picture]. 20th Century Fox.

Eightball & MJG (Artists). (1993). Pimps. Coming Out Hard [CD]. Suave Records.

Davis, B. (2008, November 5). Voters cast their ballots with the economy in mind, Exit polls indicate. Wall Street Journal - Eastern Edition, A7.

DeNavas-Walt, C., Proctor, B.D., & Smith, J. (2011). Income, poverty, and health insurance coverage in the United States: 2010. U.S. Census Bureau, Current Population Reports, p 14-22.

Destiny's Child. (Artists). (2004). Soldier. Destiny Fulfilled [CD]. Columbia Records

Federal Aviation Administration, Air Traffic Activity System (ATADS). (2012). Airport operations, Standard Report. Retrieved from https://aspm.faa.gov/opsnet/sys/Airport.asp

Flightless birds. (1997). Monkeyshines on Health & Science, 20.

Fogel, R.W. (1989) Without consent of contract: The rise and fall of American slavery. New York: W.W. Norton.

Gardner, H. (1983) Frames of mind: The theory of multiple intelligences. New York: BasicBooks, a division of HarperCollins Publishers, Inc.

Gibbs, N. (1994). Murder in miniature. (cover story). Time, 144(12), 54.

Harris, J.B. (2011). High on the hog: A culinary journey from Africa to America. New York: Bloomsbury.

Hewitt, B. (1994). Death at an early age. People, 42(12), 52.

Hoerr, J. (1988). And the wolf finally came: The decline of the American steel industry. University of Pittsburgh Press.

Isidore, C. (2012). African-American CEOs still rare. CNNMoney. Retrieved from http://money.cnn.com/2012/03/22/news/companies/black-ceo/index.htm

Jay-Z (Artist). (1999). Brooklyn's finest. Reasonable Doubt [CD]. Roc-a-Fella Records.

_____. (1998). Ride or die. Vol. 2, Hard Knock Life [CD]. Roc-a-Fella Records.

_____. (2006). 30 something. Kingdom Come [CD]. Roc-a-Fella Records

Johnson, H. (1998). Black wall street: From riot to renaissance in Tulsa's historic Greenwood district. Austin: Eakin Press

Kennedy, R. (2002) nigger: The strange career of a troublesome word. New York: Pantheon Books, a division of Random House, Inc.

Khalifa, W. (Artist), & Dogg, S. (Artist). (2011). Young, wild & free. Mac & Devin Go to High School [CD]. Atlantic Records.

Knowles, B. (Artist). (2008). Diva. I am...Sasha Fierce [CD]. Columbia Records

Lil' Wayne (Artist). (2009). Steady mobbin. We Are Young Money [CD]. Cash Money Records.

Line, L. (1994). Have wings, can't fly. International Wildlife, 24(6), 22.

Low, W.A. (1981). Encyclopedia of black America (p 144, 486-489, 698-702). New York: McGraw-Hill

Onions, C.T. (Ed.). (1966). The Oxford dictionary of English etymology. New York: Oxford University Press

McBride, J. (2007). Hip-hop Planet. National Geographic, 211(4), 100-119.

Mya (Artist) & Jay-Z (Artist). (2000). Best of me, Part 2. DJ Clue Presents: Backstage Mixtape [CD]. Roc-a-Fella Records.

Nielsen SoundScan. (2012). The Nielsen Company & Billboard's 2011 music industry report, 1-10.

Nitsche, N. S. & Brueckner, H. (2009, August 7) "Opting out of the Family? Racial Inequality in Family Formation Patterns Among Highly Educated Women"

Oates, S.B. (1982) Let the trumpet sound: A life of Martin Luther King, Jr. New York:

HarperPerennial, a division of HarperCollins Publishers, Inc.

Obama, B. H. (Speaker). (2008, November 4). Victory speech [Video]. C-SPAN Video Library. Retrieved from http://www.c-spanvideo.org/program/282164-2

Palmer, G. (1985). Tulsa's Greenwood centre was once "Black Wall Street of the – southwest'. The Daily Oklahoman.

Pew Research Center, Social and Demographic Trends. (2011, July 26) "Wealth Gaps Rise to Record Highs Between Whites, Blacks and Hispanics"

Porter, T (Artist). (2012). Make it rain. From Day 1 [CD]. RCA Records

Poussaint, A. F. (1967). How the 'white problem' spawned 'black power'. Ebony, 22(10), 88.

Rose, T. (1994). Black noise: Rap music and black culture in contemporary America. Hanover: University Press of New England.

Royce, E. (1993) The origins of southern sharecropping. Philadelphia: Temple University Press.

Spriggs, W.E. (Jan/Feb 2006). Poverty in America: The poor are getting poorer. (Undetermined) Crisis (Baltimore, MD.:2003), 14-19.

Stein, J. (Ed.). (2001). Random House Webster unabridged dictionary (2nd ed.). New York: Random House

St. Pierre, M.A. (1991). Reaganomics and its implications for African-American family life. Journal of Black Studies Vol. 21, No. 3, 325-340.

Suhyun, S., & Jingyo, S. (2011). Changing Pattern and Process of High School Dropouts between 1980s and 2000s. Educational Research Quarterly, 34(4), 3-13.

Timoney, J.F. Chief of police Miami police, d. (n.d). Disparities in drug case sentencing. FDCH Congressional Testimony.

U.S. Census Bureau. (2012). State & county Quickfacts: Robbins, IL. Retrieved from http://quickfacts.census.gov/qfd/states/17/1764616.html

U.S. Department of Education, National Center for Education Statistics. (2011). The condition of education 2011 (NCES 2011-033), Indicator 17.

U.S. Declaration of Independence. (1776). Retrieved from http://www.loc.gov/rr/program/bib/ourdocs/DeclarInd.html

U.S. Department of Justice. Bureau of Justice Statistics. (2011). Prisoners in 2010. (NCJ236096), 26

U.S. Department of Labor. (1965). Moynihan Report (The negro family: The case for national action). Retrieved from http://www.dol.gov/oasam/programs/history/webid-meynihan.htm

Valentine, V. L. (2006). Sports and Civil Rights. (Undetermined). Crisis (Baltimore, Md.: 2003), 113(6), 2.

Wiese, A. (2005). Robbins, IL. The electronic encyclopedia of Chicago. Retrieved from http://www.encyclopedia.chicagohistory.org/pages/1083.html

HarperPerennial, a division of HarperCollins Publishers, Inc.

Obama, B. H. (Speaker). (2008, November 4). Victory speech [Video]. C-SPAN Video Library. Retrieved from http://www.c-spanvideo.org/program/282164-2

Palmer, G. (1985). Tulsa's Greenwood centre was once "Black Wall Street of the – southwest'. The Daily Oklahoman.

Pew Research Center, Social and Demographic Trends. (2011, July 26) "Wealth Gaps Rise to Record Highs Between Whites, Blacks and Hispanics"

Porter, T (Artist). (2012). Make it rain. From Day 1 [CD]. RCA Records

Poussaint, A. F. (1967). How the 'white problem' spawned 'black power'. Ebony, 22(10), 88.

Rose, T. (1994). Black noise: Rap music and black culture in contemporary America. Hanover: University Press of New England.

Royce, E. (1993) The origins of southern sharecropping. Philadelphia: Temple University Press.

Spriggs, W.E. (Jan/Feb 2006). Poverty in America: The poor are getting poorer. (Undetermined) Crisis (Baltimore, MD.:2003), 14-19.

Stein, J. (Ed.). (2001). Random House Webster unabridged dictionary (2nd ed.). New York: Random House

St. Pierre, M.A. (1991). Reaganomics and its implications for African-American family life. Journal of Black Studies Vol. 21, No. 3, 325-340.

Suhyun, S., & Jingyo, S. (2011). Changing Pattern and Process of High School Dropouts between 1980s and 2000s. Educational Research Quarterly, 34(4), 3-13.

Timoney, J.F. Chief of police Miami police, d. (n.d). Disparities in drug case sentencing. FDCH Congressional Testimony.

U.S. Census Bureau. (2012). State & county Quickfacts: Robbins, IL. Retrieved from http://quickfacts.census.gov/qfd/states/17/1764616.html

U.S. Department of Education, National Center for Education Statistics. (2011). The condition of education 2011 (NCES 2011-033), Indicator 17.

U.S. Declaration of Independence. (1776). Retrieved from http://www.loc.gov/rr/program/bib/ourdocs/DeclarInd.html

U.S. Department of Justice. Bureau of Justice Statistics. (2011). Prisoners in 2010. (NCJ236096), 26

U.S. Department of Labor. (1965). Moynihan Report (The negro family: The case for national action). Retrieved from http://www.dol.gov/oasam/programs/history/webid-meynihan.htm

Valentine, V. L. (2006). Sports and Civil Rights. (Undetermined). Crisis (Baltimore, Md.: 2003), 113(6), 2.

Wiese, A. (2005). Robbins, IL. The electronic encyclopedia of Chicago. Retrieved from http://www.encyclopedia.chicagohistory.org/pages/1083.html

INDEX